Teacher Professional Development: The Critical Friends Group(CFG) Model

Nafiye Çiğdem Aktekin

Teacher Professional Development:The Critical Friends Group(CFG) Model

LAP LAMBERT Academic Publishing

Impressum / Imprint
Bibliografische Information der Deutschen Nationalbibliothek: Die Deutsche Nationalbibliothek verzeichnet diese Publikation in der Deutschen Nationalbibliografie; detaillierte bibliografische Daten sind im Internet über http://dnb.d-nb.de abrufbar.
Alle in diesem Buch genannten Marken und Produktnamen unterliegen warenzeichen-, marken- oder patentrechtlichem Schutz bzw. sind Warenzeichen oder eingetragene Warenzeichen der jeweiligen Inhaber. Die Wiedergabe von Marken, Produktnamen, Gebrauchsnamen, Handelsnamen, Warenbezeichnungen u.s.w. in diesem Werk berechtigt auch ohne besondere Kennzeichnung nicht zu der Annahme, dass solche Namen im Sinne der Warenzeichen- und Markenschutzgesetzgebung als frei zu betrachten wären und daher von jedermann benutzt werden dürften.

Bibliographic information published by the Deutsche Nationalbibliothek: The Deutsche Nationalbibliothek lists this publication in the Deutsche Nationalbibliografie; detailed bibliographic data are available in the Internet at http://dnb.d-nb.de.
Any brand names and product names mentioned in this book are subject to trademark, brand or patent protection and are trademarks or registered trademarks of their respective holders. The use of brand names, product names, common names, trade names, product descriptions etc. even without a particular marking in this works is in no way to be construed to mean that such names may be regarded as unrestricted in respect of trademark and brand protection legislation and could thus be used by anyone.

Coverbild / Cover image: www.ingimage.com

Verlag / Publisher:
LAP LAMBERT Academic Publishing
ist ein Imprint der / is a trademark of
OmniScriptum GmbH & Co. KG
Heinrich-Böcking-Str. 6-8, 66121 Saarbrücken, Deutschland / Germany
Email: info@lap-publishing.com

Herstellung: siehe letzte Seite /
Printed at: see last page
ISBN: 978-3-659-51450-0

Zugl. / Approved by: Adana, Çukurova University, Diss.,2013

Contents

Chapter 3   Results and Discussion   58

Preface

In-service training is believed to be a key factor in influencing the professional development of teachers and contributing to the improvement of their knowledge, skills and motivation. Language teachers, similar to teachers in all fields, are often encouraged to consider the importance of lifelong and on-going professional learning. Many studies in Turkey have evaluated the in-service teacher education programmes for English teachers, revealed the benefits as well as the problems encountered (Güçeri, 2005; Cimer, Çakır & Çimer, 2010; Uysal, 2012). This study investigated the impact of an in-service teacher education programme (INSET) on teachers who worked in Critical Friends Group (CFG) at Mersin University, School of Foreign Languages.

In this study, the researcher aimed at stimulating the professional development of teachers. To this end, a development-based INSET course was programmed for the instructors according to needs analysis conducted. In the first phase of the study, the attitudes and expectations of the teachers towards an INSET course were inquired. The teachers were asked to specify the areas they thought they need to improve in their teaching. The data was gathered by the means of questionnaires and interviews. Then the teachers were encouraged to join in the Critical Friends Group (CFG), which is a method where 'critical friends', who are colleagues from the same educational institution work to help each other. CFG was formed with 6 teachers and the researcher was the facilitator and the observer in the group. Protocols were used in the meetings. Each protocol cycles was organised by the researcher and the group was informed about the procedure thoroughly. The second phase of the study was the organization and the implementation of the INSET course. The last phase of the study was the evaluation of the data. Data came from the journals participant teachers kept, meeting transcripts, interviews and questionnaires held, and from the researcher's notes.

In this study, the researcher aimed to find out the attitudes and expectations of the instructors at Foreign Languages School of Mersin University concerning the effects of development-based INSET programme, the areas the teachers think they need training and development. How INSET programme followed by the Critical Friends Group (CFG) affected their professional development, and whether CFG was proved to be an efficient tool to evaluate the process teachers go through before and after the INSET were investigated. The attitudes and expectations of the teachers after the INSET programme were also evaluated.

The results of the study showed that the teachers who worked in CFG benefited from this inquiry-based model of professional development, and the INSET programme followed by a CFG contributed to their practices. The findings are meant to guide INSET programmes for directions in which needs analysis are taken into account, and more teacher involvement is provided.

Nafiye Çiğdem AKTEKİN
Supervisor: Prof. Dr. Zuhal OKAN
Çukurova University, TURKEY
May, 2013

v

Acknowledgements

I want to extend my sincere gratitude to the many people who supported me along my doctoral journey. The contribution of these people in different ways made it possible to write this thesis. I would like to express my greatest gratitude to Prof. Dr. Zuhal Okan, the supervisor of my doctoral dissertation, for her support and encouragement throughout the writing of this thesis.

I would like to thank to Asst. Prof. Rana Yıldırım and Assoc. Prof. Ergün Serindağ for their valuable comments and understanding. Their participation in the dissertation committee was a source of encouragement and guidance. I owe special thanks to Asst. Prof. Gülden İlin for her valuable comments, and I am grateful to Asst. Prof. Yıldız Turgut for her invaluable feedback, support, and guidance. I am also indebted to the professors in the Department of English Language Teaching at Çukurova University for their dedication, professionalism and inspiration during my doctoral courses.

I am grateful to the participant instructors, my dear colleagues, Aslı Güler Tülgen, Aynur Yüksel, Selvin Güven, Suna Aksoy Gürbüz, Şayeste Önder Dora, and Tuğba Gürsoy Dinç for their voluntary participation, contributions, and unceasing effort and support throughout the study. Without their support and enthusiasm, I would not have completed this thesis. I wish to express my appreciation to my student and colleague-to-be, Mehtap Topak, for supporting me and helping out with the transcription of the journals, and Yalçın Serttaş for the transcription of the audiotapes. You are going to be great teachers!

Finally, a heartfelt thank you goes to my family; to my husband Mustafa; the most wonderful partner a person could have, and to my lovely and amazing sons, Kerem and Alp, who allowed me the time and the space, in their young lives, to do this work and to pursue this path. "I love you so much!" I am also grateful to my mother, Sıdıka Koçak, and my father Kemal Koçak, for encouraging me and supporting me all my life. They have always believed in me, which has been the source of my success, and motivation. I count among my greatest fortunes that I am surrounded by these wonderful people. Thank you all.

List of Abbreviations

AISR	: Annenberg Institute for School Reform
CES	: Coalition of Essential Schools
CFG	: Critical Friends Group
CTD	: Collaborative Teacher Development
ELT	: English Language Learning
INSET	: In-service Teacher Education
NSRF	: National School Reform Faculty
PLC	: Professional Learning Communities
SCT	: Sociocultural Theory
TPD	: Teacher Professional Development

List of Tables

List of Figures

List of Appendices

Introduction: Teacher Professional Development

In the present time, the English language skills of a good proportion of its citizenry are seen essential for most of the countries. Participating in the global economy, being part of a world of academy, culture, technology all requires knowing English. Therefore, English teaching and English language teachers are at the heart of this need.

Language teaching is very dynamic in nature, so as English language teaching. In order to meet the demands of the changing world, an effective teacher needs to be aware of the changes in teaching methods and approaches and reflect these in her teaching as much as possible. In most schools and institutions today, language teachers are expected to keep up to date with developments in the field, to regularly review and evaluate their teaching skills, and to take on new teaching assignments according to the changing needs of the institution (Richards & Farrell, 2005). The necessity of on-going and lifelong professional learning has been emphasized for in-service teachers by the researchers (England, 1998; Theunissen & Veenman, 1998; Crandall, 2000; Zeichner & Noffke, 2001; Crandall, personal communication, 11 July, 2012). However, current in-service education and training programmes (INSET) are often found to be unsatisfactory due to the fact that they do not provide the teachers with opportunities to be actively involved in their development and to reflect on their teaching experiences (Atay, 2008). Teachers gain from training courses if the benefits of reflective approaches, in which the views and feelings of a learner play a main role in the success of second language acquisition pedagogy, and student-teacher relationships are highlighted (Saito & Ebsworth, 2004).

During the past decade, a considerable body of literature and research has emerged on teacher professional development, teacher learning and teacher change. The research literature contains large and small-scale studies, including intensive case studies of classroom teaching, evaluations of specific approaches to improving teaching and learning, and surveys of teachers about their pre-service preparation and in-service professional development (Garet et al., 2001). Despite all the literature and the studies, however, relatively little systematic research has been conducted on the effects of professional development on improvements in teaching or on student outcomes. These research studies have tried to determine the efficacy of various types of professional development activities. Studies that are extended over time, across broad teacher learning communities, and designed by teachers, not to teachers, reveal relatively more realistic and systematic outcomes.

For the professional development of teachers, in-service training programmes have been applied as a method of increasing the knowledge, skills, and positive beliefs of teachers. England (1998) explains that teachers are the educators of others, therefore, 'intrinsically want and need to participate in on-going development and change in their own professional lives.' Several studies showed that INSETs have confidence-building effect on teachers because INSETs help teachers not only raise awareness on pedagogic issues but also develop their personal qualities (Freeman, 1982; Güçeri, 2005; Şahin, 2006). However, traditionally the professional development of teachers has been thought of something that is done by others for or to teachers, and most training programmes are considered to be general rather than specific. Teachers are passive listeners; the programmes lack effective models; they generally do not have any provision for feedback and they lack follow-up process. Studies reveal the fact that teachers generally consider that in-service training activities are planned with insufficient relevance to their particular classroom practices and realities of their classrooms (Şeker, 2007; Atay, 2009; Bayrakçı, 2009). Therefore, in-service training needs of teachers should be considered, and teachers should have the opportunity to have a word in their own professional development.

In recent years, there has been a shift which changes the direction of staff development. There is a shift from transmission, product-oriented theories to constructivist, process-oriented theories of learning. From constructivist point of view, learners construct their own knowledge by looking for meaning and order; they interpret what they hear, read, and see based on their previous learning and habits; they take responsibility for their own learning. According to Crandall (2000), teacher development is a life-long process of growth which may involve collaborative and/or autonomous learning, but the important distinction is that teachers are engaged in the process and they actively reflect on their practices. Teachers can plan many aspects of their own professional learning; can decide what kind of support they will need, can select a colleague or colleagues to work with, can set realistic goals and establish a time frame and evaluate what they have learned and share the results with others (Richards & Farrell, 2005). Many education experts advocate for teacher-directed professional development experiences that foster a professional learning community (Darling-Hammond & Sykes, 2004). According to Crandall (personal communication, 11 July, 2012), the most effective professional development of teachers begins with their concerns and their classroom. Teachers are engaged in "teacher talk" much of the day around specific areas of concern that are unique to each teacher. Professional development models that allow teachers to "talk" about their concerns have been linked to widespread school change (Little, Gearhart, Curry, & Kafta, 2003; Allen & Blythe, 2004). Moreover, teacher learning has socially situated nature, and teachers learn more in specific classrooms and school situations. Effective professional development involves teachers in talking with another. Therefore, collaboration in school environment has proved to be effective both for teachers and students. Collaboration as a model of professional development impacts instructional practice and improves student achievement outcomes. Therefore, teachers should be supported to work in collaborative groups to reconstruct their professional knowledge (Şeker, 2007).

Collaborative teacher development (CTD) is an increasingly common kind of teacher development found in a wide range of language teaching contexts. Teaching has no longer viewed as an occupation pursued in isolation from one's colleagues as Freeman (1998) described it as an "egg-box profession" in which each of us is kept separate from our fellow teachers. An important component of teacher development has been to overcome this isolation with collaborative endeavours both within and beyond the classroom. CTD can take different forms framed within various approaches to teacher development. Action research, narrative inquiry, cooperative development, exploratory practice, team teaching, teacher study groups, critical friends group, dialog journal writing, long-distance collaboration are some of these.

The Critical Friends Group model of reflective practice and professional development has its roots in three school reform networks; the Coalition of Essential Schools (CES), the Annenberg Institute for School Reforms (AISR), and the National School Reform Faculty (NSFR). Dissatisfied with typical forms of professional development, educators from all three organizations developed an approach that was focused on teacher practice, was teacher driven, and promoted professional collegiality

(Anderson & Hudson, 2002). A Critical Friend Group (CFG) was defined as "a professional learning community consisting of approximately eight to twelve educators who come together voluntarily at least once a month for about two hours. The phrase 'critical friend' has been in use since 1970s within the context of school self-appraisal. As Costa and Kallick (1993) defines, a critical friend is '…a trusted person who asks provocative questions, provides data to be examined through another lens, and offers critiques of a person's work as a friend. A critical friend takes the time to fully understand the context of the work presented and the outcomes that the person or group is working toward. The friend is an advocate for the success of that work'. A CFG is composed of peers where there is no 'hierarchy of expertise' and it must support a democratic, reflective, and collaborative community of learners (McKenzie & Carr-Reardon, 2003). Group members are committed to improving their practice through collaborative learning" (NSFR website). The CFG process acknowledges the complex art of teaching and provides structures for teachers to improve their teaching by giving and receiving feedback (Bambino, 2002). CFG allows its members to help each other to examine their own work and make changes whenever required. As Johnson (2009) stated, consistent with a socio-cultural perspective, CFG model seeks to create a mediational space for teachers to engage in on-going, in-depth, systematic, and reflective examinations of their teaching practices and their students' learning.

With CFG model, the researcher aimed at evaluating the impact of an INSET programme which was planned according to the needs of the participants. Additionally, an on-going, reflective and collaborative form of teachers' professional development was aimed to be created. CFG was also the tool to provide effective feedback and strong support for the teachers in their classroom and social practices. CFG was implemented for teachers with teachers, contrary to traditional forms of training programmes. The researcher tried to consider that teachers are adult learners who learn in different ways, come from different backgrounds, work in a variety of settings, and cater for the needs of diverse students. Teachers have individual needs, different motivations for learning, and prior knowledge and experience that will impact on the type of learning they choose to engage in. This researcher believes that the professional development initiative, CFGs, shows substantial promise for addressing these needs.

An INSET programme can address training or development needs of teachers (Roberts, 1998). While training is characterized by objectives that are defined by a deficit in language teaching skills, curricular knowledge or some other areas of expertise (p.221), professional development is career orientated and has a narrower, more instrumental and utilitarian remit (Mann, 2005). In this study, development inside a training programme was encouraged, teachers' needs were taken into account, and a teacher professional development approach within an inquiry-based model was preferred. Moreover, the teachers were encouraged to work in the CFG, which was the vehicle for instituting collaborative efforts in order to evaluate the outcomes of the INSET and to foster professional development. This study also aimed to promote teacher collaboration. Teacher collaboration helps teachers to rethink disciplinary knowledge as well as their teaching strategies. School-based inquiry promotes effective dialogue and discussion among staff that leads to a teaching, learning environment. The notion that teachers can develop as participants in professional learning communities has been discussed in the relation to the sociocultural theory.

Through a development-based INSET programme, participant teachers in the school were expected to explore their own professional development, as well as to foster peer development by the help of CFG. For the purpose of the study, five sets of questions were asked:

1. What are the attitudes and expectations of Turkish EFL teachers at Foreign Languages School of Mersin University concerning the effects of development-based INSET programme?
2. In what areas do the teachers think they need training and development?
3. In their own view, how has INSET programme followed by the Critical Friends Group (CFG) affected their professional development?
4. Has CFG proved to be an efficient tool to evaluate the process teachers go through before and after the INSET? If yes, how?
5. Is there any change in teachers' expectations about language teaching and learning after the INSET programme?

Definitions of Terms

The following terms were used for this study:

Collaborative Teacher Development (CTD): Collaboration is a style of interaction between at least two coequal parties voluntarily engaged in shared decision making as they work toward a common goal (Cook & Friend, 1995). Collaborative Teacher Development arises from, and reinforces, a view of teacher learning as a fundamentally social process- in other words, that teachers can only learn professionally in sustained and meaningful ways when they are able to do so together (Johnston, 2009). CTD arises from a belief that teaching can and should be a fundamentally collegial profession.

Collegiality: Collegiality indicates more than supportive relationships among teachers; rather, it indicates a professional community with norms of innovation and learning, where teachers are enthusiastic about their work, and where focus is upon devising strategies that enable all students to prosper (McLaughlin, 1992). Important factors in collegial professional communities are capacity for reflection, feedback, and problem solving.

Critical Friends Group (CFG): A CFG is a professional learning community consisting of approximately 8-12 educators who come together voluntarily at least once a month for about 2 hours. Group members are committed to improving their practice through collaborative learning. In CFG context, critical means "important," "key," "essential," or "urgent" such as in "critical care." Furthermore, when a group of educators develop a CFG, they begin by spending time discussing and developing norms about how to give feedback and how to question in a sensitive manner so that everyone feels comfortable. Trust and confidentiality are established among participants.

INSET (In-service Teacher Training): INSET can be defined as education and training activities engaged in by teachers and directors, following their initial professional certification, and intended primarily or exclusively to improve their professional knowledge, skills and attitudes in order that they can educate learners of all ages more effectively. More recently, the Education Information Network in the European Union (EURYDICE) has defined in-service training as 'a variety of activities and practices in which teachers become involved in order to broaden their knowledge, improve their skills and assess and develop their professional approach' (Perron, 1991, cited in Bayrakci, 2009).

National School Reform Faculty (NSRF): The National School Reform Faculty (NSRF) is a professional development initiative that focuses on increasing student achievement through professional learning communities called Critical Friends Groups, or CFGs. The NSRF was developed from the programme founded by the Annenberg Institute for School Reform in 1995.

Teacher Professional Development (TPD): Professional development refers to the development of a person in his or her professional role. Teacher development is the professional growth a teacher achieves as a result of gaining increased experience and examining his or her teaching systematically (Glatthorn, 1995; cited in Villegas-

Reimers, 2003). Teacher professional development is now seen as a long-term process that includes regular opportunities and experiences planned systematically to promote growth and development in the profession.

Professional Learning Communities (PLC): A group of teachers who regularly gather together to share their expertise while collaborating on specific tasks with the goal of improving their teaching practice. Fullan & Stiegelbauer (1991) defines learning communities as a teacher-workplace where innovation and improvement are built into the daily activities of teachers.

Protocols: Structured processes developed by the Annenberg Institute for School Reform to guide group conversation as teachers collectively examine student work and discuss concerns relative to student learning. CFG are built around the use of protocol-guided conversations. Protocols set rules for who speaks, when, and about what, in essence framing the discourse.

Reflective Practice: Reflective practice is a process in which participants can develop a greater level of self-awareness about the nature and impact of their performance, an awareness that creates opportunities for professional growth and development. Schön (1983) suggested that the capacity to reflect on action so as to engage in a process of continuous learning was one of the defining characteristics of professional practice.

Sociocultural Theory: Lev Vygotsky, a Russian psychologist, first wrote about sociocultural theory in the 1920s. He believed that people do not interact directly with the environment, but that these interactions are always and everywhere mediated. These mediations could take place either through cultural artifacts (such as physical tools and symbols) or by other human beings through discourse (Poehner, 2009). Sociocultural theory ascertains that people do not exist in isolation, but are constantly interacting with others and the environment to develop higher orders of thinking and being. In addition, Vygotsky claims that the knowledge of an individual is constructed through the knowledge of the social group to which the individual belongs.

Sociocultural Perspective: Learning to teach, from sociocultural perspective, is based on the assumption that knowing, thinking and understanding come from participating in the social practices of learning and teaching in specific classroom and school situations (Johnson, 2009; 13). As for Johnson, it shifts the focus of attention onto teachers as learners of L2 teaching and it highlights the socially situated nature of teacher learning (p.16).

Tuning Protocol: It is a formal protocol used in order for teachers to get help from colleagues on a particular issue or problem or to improve a lesson plan. The protocol usually includes a teacher presenting an issue, colleagues asking, clarifying, and then probing questions, reflection time for colleagues, discussion among colleagues (presenter does not take part of the discussion, she only listens and takes notes), presenter responds to discussion, and finally, the entire group debriefs the process (Nefstead, 2009).

Chapter 1 Review of Literature

Teacher Education and Development

It is prevalent for teaching to be considered as a 'profession' and for teachers to consider themselves as 'professional people' (Wallace, 1991), thus the English teacher is essentially a professional engaged in bringing about real-world change, who may on occasion undertake academic research (Ur, 2002). There are many key terms defining language teacher development, such as teacher training, teacher education, teacher development, professional development, continuing professional development (CPD) and staff development. Mann (2005) states that it is difficult to sustain watertight boundaries, but there are some important differences in emphasis. The core feature of this study is that it places teachers' self-development at the centre of a definition of language teacher development.

According to Crandall (2000), traditional language teacher education has involved a delicate balancing act between education and training. The former addresses the development of language knowledge and language teaching and learning. The latter emphasizes the development of skills to apply this knowledge in the practice of language teaching, with a limited opportunity to observe and practice that theory in actual classrooms or simulated contexts such as microteaching. Richards and Farrell (2005) define training as activities directly focused on teacher's present responsibilities and are typically aimed at short-term and immediate goals. Training involves understanding basic concepts and principles as a prerequisite for applying them to teaching and the ability to demonstrate principles and practices in the classroom (p. 3). Development, on the other hand, generally refers to general growth not focused on a specific job, serving a longer term goal and facilitating growth of teachers' understanding of teaching and of themselves as teachers (Richard & Farrell, 2005, p.4).

Teacher training is sometimes considered as teacher education. Widdowson (1997) describes teacher training as solution-oriented, with the "…implication that teachers are to be given specific instruction in practical techniques to cope with predictable events..," while teacher education is problem-oriented, with the implication of "…a broader intellectual awareness of theoretical principles underlying particular practices" (1997, p.121). In both orientations, the prospective or experienced teacher is viewed as a passive recipient of transmitted knowledge; omitted is any understanding of the role that language teachers play in their own development, which teacher research has begun to demonstrate as being of considerable importance (Edge & Richards 1993, Woodward 1991). Teacher development is a life-long process of growth which may involve collaborative and/or autonomous learning, but the important distinction is that teachers are engaged in the process and they actively reflect on their practices. According to Wallace (1991), "the distinction is that training or education is something that can be presented or managed by others; whereas development is something that can be done only by and for oneself" (p.3).

Lastly, from a humanistic and psychological point of view, Underhill (1999) defines teacher development as "one version of personal development [...] personal development as a teacher". He says he sees "the process of development as the process of increasing our conscious choices about the way we think, feel and behave as a teacher. It is about the inner world of responses that we make to the outer world of the classroom. Development is seen as a process of becoming increasingly aware of the quality of the learning atmosphere we create, and as a result becoming more able to make creative moment by moment choices about how we are affecting our learners through our personal behaviour (Underhill, 1999).

Freeman (2001) gives the overview of teacher training and teacher development and mentions that there are misconceptions that tend to surround these two strategies. The first misconception is that they are often presented as dichotomous and mutually exclusive, which they are not (p.76). According to him, both training and development depend on information which is external to teacher-learners, which they incorporate through internal processes into their own thinking and practice. Another misconception is that training and development are often couched in sequential terms. Freeman states that although it is true training tends to be a pre-service strategy, while development is more widely used in in-service contexts, the most effective L2 teacher education programmes blend the two.

The importance of teacher development has been the focus of attention in the field of language teaching, and language teachers are often encouraged to consider the need of lifelong and on-going professional learning. Mann (2005) argues that the distinction between professional development and teacher development is not that marked in the literature but is worth considering. Professional development is career orientated, and has a narrower, more instrumental and utilitarian remit, whereas teacher development is more inclusive of personal and moral dimensions (Mann, 2005). He summaries the core themes in teacher development as:

Language teacher development

- is a bottom–up process and as such can be contrasted with top–down staff development programmes;
- values the insider view rather than the outsider view;
- is independent of the organization but often functioning more successfully with its support and recognition;
- is a continuing process of becoming and can never be finished;
- is a process of articulating an inner world of conscious choices made in response to the outer world of the teaching context;
- is wider than professional development and includes personal, moral and value dimensions;
- can be encouraged and integrated in both training and education programmes (p.105).

Development of teaching competence is our professional responsibility, and we can undertake a wide range of activities in fulfilment of this obligation (Pettis, 2002), and there are courses to take, journals to read, colleagues to talk with and observe, classroom research to conduct, textbooks to review, and workshops to attend. According to Richards and Farrell (2005), teachers need regular opportunities to update their professional knowledge and skills, and they can do this by being able to take part in activities such as:

- engaging in self-reflection and evaluation,
- developing specialized knowledge and skills about many aspects of teaching,
- expanding their knowledge base about research, theory and issues in teaching,
- taking on new roles and responsibilities, such as supervisor or mentor teacher, teacher-researcher, or materials writer,
- developing collaborative relationships with other teachers. (p.vii)

First and foremost of all is that as educators we must make a personal commitment to our own on-going professional growth. It should be kept in mind that the need for on-going renewal of professional skills and knowledge is not a reflection of inadequate training but simply a response to the fact that not everything teachers need to know can be provided at pre-service level, as well as the fact that the knowledge base of teaching constantly changes (Richards & Farrell, 2005). Change is a necessary part of teacher development.

Models of Teacher Education

Wallace (1991) identifies three major models of language teacher education: 1) a craft or apprenticeship model by which less experienced teachers learn through observing those with more experience; 2) an applied science or theory-to-practice model by which knowledge is learned from experts and then applied in real-world contexts; and 3) a reflective model by which teachers reflect upon, evaluate, and adapt their own practice. These three models broadly correspond to the three views of teaching identified by Freeman (1991; 1996): 1) teaching as doing (a behavioural model emphasizing what teachers do and encouraging a skills or craft model of teacher education); 2) teaching as thinking and doing (a cognitive model emphasizing what teachers know and how they do it, encouraging both theory and skills development and craft and applied science models of teacher education); and 3) teaching as knowing what to do (an interpretivist view emphasizing why teachers do what they do in different contexts, encouraging the addition of reflection and the development of frameworks of interpretation to theory and skill development in teacher education).

Crandall (2000) states that these three models of language teacher education Wallace introduced are likely to be needed in all teacher development but in different degrees depending upon teacher experience and understanding. However, neither traditional education nor training is sufficient; opportunities for teachers to reflect upon their beliefs and practices and to construct and reconstruct their personal theories of language teaching and learning are also needed (Bailey 1992, Freeman and Richards 1996). Teaching depends upon the application of appropriate theory, the development of careful instructional designs and strategies, and the study of what actually happens in the classroom (Richards 1990).

The core of traditional language teacher education has long been the methods course, a course which presents the theoretical rationale and practical implications of language teaching approaches, methods, procedures, and techniques (Blair 1982, Richards & Rodgers 1982, Larsen-Freeman 1986, Celce-Murcia 1991, Stevick 1980). Methods courses often discuss the rationale of "innovative" methods (e.g., Silent Way,

Community Language Learning, Natural Approach, Content-based Language Instruction) as well as "traditional" ones (Grammar-Translation, Audio-Lingual, Communicative), and they often combine this discussion with specific attention to techniques for teaching the four skills (listening, speaking, reading, and writing).

As Crandall (2000) states, while courses in language teaching methods are still central to language teacher education, there is growing concern that they not be taught in prescriptivist terms, as recipes or cookbooks for effective teaching. Rather, they need to investigate the range of instructional options language teachers have available in their repertoires and, through case studies, interviews, or introspection, examine the kinds of decisions teachers make in planning and carrying out instruction (Richards 1990, Roberts 1998, Stevick 1998, William & Burden 1997). The shift from methods to methodology is consonant with constructivist theories of learning—a shift away from a top-down approach to methods as "products" for teachers to learn and "match" and toward a bottom-up approach to methodology as reflections on experiences. The shift involves prospective teachers in "…exploring the nature of effective teaching and learning, and discovering the strategies used by successful teachers and learners in the classroom" (Richards 1990).

In describing and analysing their model to enhance teacher development Bell and Gilbert (1996) highlight three main aspects:

1. Learning as purposeful inquiry. The teachers investigating different aspects of teaching that are viewed as problematic and that they wish to change.
2. Social, personal and professional development. Involving collaborative work to reconstruct the socially agreed knowledge; attending to individual ideas, values and feelings to reconstruct personal knowledge; and changing conceptions and beliefs about teaching as well as classroom activities and practices.
3. Empowerment of the teacher for on-going self-development, rather than one of continued dependency on a facilitator to act on their world.

Teacher development may occur when teachers are encouraged to reflect upon new ideas, activities and perspectives; when they have opportunities and support to put such ideas into practice, to reflect in and on their practices, alongside a skilful critical friend; when teachers work collaboratively and get proper support to realize that new approaches work and are worthwhile. As Kelchtermans (1994) stated we "do not have the illusion that it is possible to develop an all-encompassing theoretical framework, with clear prescriptions about how to operate in teacher training. But this should not prevent us from trying to integrate partial and fragmented research results, well established training practices and our own professional reflection into larger entities".

Teacher Professional Development

Teacher professional development is about teachers learning, learning how to learn, and transforming their knowledge into practice for the benefit of their students' growth. According to Avalos (2011) teacher professional learning is a complex process, which requires cognitive and emotional involvement of teachers individually and collectively, the capacity and willingness to examine where each one stands in terms of convictions and beliefs and the perusal and enactment of appropriate alternatives for improvement or change. She also adds that this occurs in particular educational policy environments or school cultures, some of which are more appropriate and conducive to learning than others. The instruments used to trigger development also depend on the objectives and needs of teachers as well as of their students (Avalos, 2011, p.11). Attending formal structures such as courses, workshops, INSET programmes can serve some purposes. Informal structures such as producing the curricula, discussing the assessment results, or sharing some ideas and strategies may serve other purposes. Therefore, as Fullan (2007) argued professional development is 'the sum total of formal and informal learning experiences throughout one's career.'

Teachers' teaching career requires constant upgrading, improvement and development. Thus, teachers' needs may differ from one stage to others in their life-long learning continuum. Huberman (2001) defines and identifies five stages of teacher professional development from the beginning to their retirement as follows:

- Career entry (1-3 years in the profession): Teachers try to survive and discover their job;
- Stabilisation (4-6 years in the profession): Teachers show their commitment;
- Divergent period (8-18 years in the profession): Teachers explore themselves and develop new methods of teaching;

- Second divergent period (19-30 years in the profession): Some teacher relax and assess themselves, others criticize the system, administration, colleagues, and so on;
- Disengagement (up to 50 years of experience): Teachers gradually separate from their profession; some other teachers find it a time of bitterness.

Teachers are at the core of any teaching and learning process and teacher professionalism must increase if education is to improve. Skilful, knowledgeable and enthusiastic teachers can form a foundation of good schools with high quality students. When the stages Huberman argued are considered, teachers need life-long investment in their jobs. Enhancing teachers' teaching career is considered the most important and strategic investments of time, money and efforts that human resource managers make in education (Holland, 2005).

Models for Teacher Professional Development

There are number of models that have been developed and implemented to promote and support teachers' professional development. Teacher professional development (TPD) is the instruction provided to teachers to promote their development in a certain area. According to Gaible and Burns (2005), it is the tool by which policymakers' visions for change are disseminated and conveyed to teachers. Though the recipient of TPD is the teacher, the ultimate beneficiary is the student.

According to Gaible and Burns (2005), TPD can be divided into three broad categories:

1- Standardized TPD

The most centralized approach, best used to disseminate information and skills among large teacher populations

2- Site-based TPD

Intensive learning by groups of teachers in a school or region, promoting profound and long-term changes in instructional methods

3- Self-directed TPD

Independent learning, sometimes initiated at the learner's discretion, using available resources that may include computers and the Internet.

Standardized TPD typically represents a centralized approach involving workshops and training sessions. Standardized, training-based approaches generally focus on the exploration of new concepts and the demonstration and modelling of skills. When employed in accordance with best practices standardized approaches can effectively:

1- Expose teachers to new ideas, new ways of doing things and new colleagues
2- Disseminate knowledge and instructional methods to teachers throughout a country or region
3- Visibly demonstrate the commitment of a nation or vendor or project to a particular course of action

Gaible & Burns (2005, p.25)

Site based TPD often takes place in schools, resource centres or educational institutions. Teachers work with local ("in house") facilitators or master teachers to engage in more gradual processes of learning, building master of pedagogy, content and technology skills. Site based TPD often focuses on the specific, situational problems that individual teachers encounter as they try to implement new techniques in their classroom practices. According to Gaible and Burns (2005, p.26) site-based models tend to:

- Bring people together to address local issues and needs over a period of time
- Encourage individual initiative and collaborative approaches to problems
- Allow more flexible, sustained and intensive TPD
- Provide on-going opportunities for professional learning among a single set of teachers.

Lastly, in self-directed TPD, teachers are involved in initiating and designing their own professional development and would share materials and ideas as well as discuss challenges and solutions.

Villegas-Reimers (2003) groups models in two sections; organizational partnership models and small groups and individual models. The first section describes models that require and imply certain organizational or institutional partnerships in order to be effective. Models in the second section can be implemented on a smaller scale, and they have been identified as techniques rather than models of professional development. Table 2 demonstrates the teacher professional development models

Table 2 Models of Teacher Professional Development

Organizational partnership models	Small groups or individual models
Professional- development schools	Supervision: traditional and clinical
Other university- school partnerships	Students' performance assessment
Other inter-institutional collaborations	Workshops, seminars, courses, etc.
Schools' networks	Cased-based study
Teachers' networks	Self-directed development
Distance education	Co-operative or collegial development
	Observation of excellent practice
	Teachers' participation in new roles
	Skills-development model
	Reflective models
	Project-based models
	Portfolios
	Action research
	Use of teachers' narratives
	Generational or cascade model
	Coaching/mentoring

(OECD Report; Villegas-Reimers, 2003)

Avalos (2011) points out that not every form of professional development, even those with the greatest evidence of positive impact, is of itself relevant to all teachers. There is thus a constant need to study, experiment, discuss and reflect in dealing with teacher professional development on the interacting links and influences of the history and traditions of groups of teachers, the educational needs of their student populations, the expectations of their education systems, teachers' working conditions and the opportunities to learn that are open to them (Avalos, 2011, p.10).

What is Effective Professional Development?

"It has been said that who have been teaching for twenty years may be divided into two categories: those with twenty years' experience and those with one year's experience repeated twenty times." (Ur, 1996)

Being a professional in every area is an endeavour, a purposeful or industrious undertaking. The best ways to help others and ourselves as professionals have changed considerably. As Crandall (personal communication, 11 July, 2012) has suggested it is an exciting time to be an English language teaching professional because not only have traditional opportunities for professional learning increased, but the options have expanded with the Internet and the proliferation of Web tools: e.g., blogs, wikis, online courses, webinars, podcasts, study circles, e-portfolios and numerous other social networking tools. To become a better-informed ESL professional, a number of resources are available to stimulate new ideas and reconsider the old ones. However, although teachers generally support high standards for teaching and learning, many teachers are not prepared to implement teaching practices based on high standards (Garet et. al., 2001). Many teachers learn to teach using a model of teaching and learning in their pre-service education, usually with an applied science model, which focuses heavily on memorizing facts, without emphasizing deeper understanding of subject knowledge. Shifting to a more balanced approach to teaching means that teachers must learn more about the subjects they teach, and how students learn these subjects. The continual deepening of knowledge and skills is an integral part of any profession and teaching is no exception.

Praia (1998, as cited in Miguens 1999), on the other hand, stresses some common erroneous ideas about teacher education. His examples of these mistakes are: a) that the most important is that teachers know well the content of their teaching, as well as the theory about the art of good teaching; and b) that teacher education has to be organized and oriented by teacher educators with authority to direct it from above. He points out that there is a research-based consensus on fruitful teacher education, namely:

- Teacher education programmes which give teachers opportunities to carry out collaborative work and to develop autonomy to learn, appear to be rather stimulating and productive;

- Teacher education programmes that regard the teacher as a creative professional who discusses and negotiates the goals, that devises strategies and proposes agendas and activities, that selects materials and develops innovative ideas, seem to be more successful.

- Teacher education programmes that give relevance to supervised and supported experiences and activities with appropriate feedback, work better than those that only prescribe behaviours or competencies.

What teachers learn (or do not learn) in traditional professional activities has been an area of debate for some time. Many educators still emphasize the features of effective professional development. The explanation of best professional development during 25 years has not changed considerably. For example, Little (1988; cited in Wilson & Berne, 1999) nominates the following features of effective staff development: (a) It ensures collaboration adequate to produce shared understanding, shared investment, thoughtful development, and a fair, rigorous test of selected ideas; (b) it requires collective participation in training and implementation; (c) it is focused on crucial problems of curriculum and instruction; (d) it is conducted often enough and long enough to ensure progressive gains in knowledge, skill, and confidence; and (e) it is congruent with and contributes to professional habits and norms of collegiality and experimentation. Abdal-Haqq (1995, as cited in Wilson & Berne 1999) nominates a similar set of characteristics, claiming that effective professional development

- is on-going
- includes training, practice, and feedback; opportunities for individual reflection and group inquiry into practice; and coaching or other follow-up procedures
- is school based and embedded in teacher work
- is collaborative, providing opportunities for teachers to interact with peers
- focuses on student learning which should guide assessment of its effectiveness
- encourages and supports school-based and teacher initiatives
- is rooted in the knowledge base for teaching
- incorporates constructivist approaches to teaching and learning
- recognizes teachers as professionals and adult learners
- provides adequate time and follow-up support
- is accessible and inclusive (p. 175).

The most effective professional development begins with your concerns and your classroom (Crandall, personal communication, 11 July, 2012). Professional development for language teachers should be relevant to your particular needs because all teachers have unique attributes and areas of need related to teaching practice. An experienced teacher is more likely to have different needs and interests than a novice teacher. It is also prevalent that teachers may have a preference for professional development that involves engaging with other teachers or they may prefer independent professional learning. It can also be said that some teachers seek out a balance of each type of professional development.

Richardson and Orphano (2009; cited in Crandall, personal communication, 11 July, 2012) defined effective professional development as that which improves teachers' knowledge and instructional practices as well as accelerates students' learning. They noted that sustained, content-focused professional development was most effective when it involved teachers actively and in concrete ways and concentrated on specific instructional practices rather than abstract discussions of teaching. The best professional development:

- involves learning opportunities over an extended period of time,

- engages teachers in deepening and extending skills,

- challenges teachers' assumptions about learning,

- involves teachers in talking with another,

- focuses on student learning (e.g., with groups of teachers analysing student work samples together and seeking to understand how students process information),

- has administrative support,

- is "job-embedded", i.e., immediately applicable to one's teaching practice (p.5)

When the conditions for effective professional development are considered, Nieto (2009) points out that an important condition of professional development "is a climate of openness, shared decision making, and collaboration in the school," all of which are fostered in an environment where teachers are empowered to develop, implement and reflect upon topics that interest them and relate directly to their instructional and intellectual needs (p.11). The formation of teacher teams, such as those required by collaborative professional development models, serves to combat the sense of frustration and feelings of isolation that grow when teachers do not have supportive and reflective collaborative partners. This leads us to look at the issue from a sociocultural point of view. The processes of learning to teach, according to Johnson (2009), are socially negotiated since teachers' knowledge of teaching is constructed through experiences in and with students, parents, colleagues, and administrative.

Therefore, for an effective professional development, L2 teacher education should also be evaluated from a sociocultural perspective.

A Sociocultural Perspective on L2 Teacher Education

Sociocultural theory originated in the writings of Lev Vygotsky in the early 1920's, and despite his short research career, his writings continue to influence many disciplines in the humanities and social sciences. Vygotsky and his colleagues maintained that individuals learn and develop not by following a pre-specified series of developmental stages but through mediated experiences. He claims that the knowledge of an individual occurs (i.e., is constructed) through the knowledge of the social group to which the individual belongs (Vygotsky, 1978).

In their professional practice, teachers are social beings in that they interact with their learners, the curriculum in the classroom, teaching materials and tasks. Classroom, school, the local community, country and the international community are the layers of the social context the teachers are part of. Learning to teach, from sociocultural perspective, is based on the assumption that knowing, thinking and understanding come from participating in the social practices of learning and teaching in specific classroom and school situations (Johnson, 2009, p.13). Moreover, Johnson adds that, from a sociocultural perspective, teacher learning and activities of teaching are understood as growing out of participation in the social practices in classrooms; and what teachers know and how they use that knowledge in classrooms is highly interpretative and contingent on knowledge of self, setting, students, curriculum, and community (p.13).

While designing courses, how human learning is emergent through social interactions, and where context and identity play crucial mediating roles should not be ignored. This means understanding how teacher learning emerges in the life of the classroom, staffroom and the school. Taking up a sociocultural perspective on L2 teacher education refocuses our orientation toward the professional development of L2 teachers (Johnson, 2009). As for Johnson, first and foremost, it shifts the focus of attention onto teachers as learners of L2 teaching and secondly, it highlights the socially situated nature of teacher learning. Third, it exposes the existing mediational means that shape teacher learning and it provides us with a window into how alternative mediational means may have the potential to shape it (p.16). Johnson (2009) also adds that this perspective shows us how teacher learning not only shapes how teachers think and act but how changes in teachers' ways of thinking and acting have the potential to change students' ways of engaging in activities which can in turn change their ways of learning as well as what they learn. Finally, a sociocultural perspective is not a methodology or approach to how to "do" L2 teacher education. Instead, it is a theoretical lens, a mindset or way of conceptualizing teacher learning that informs how L2 teacher educators understand and support the professional development of L2 teachers (Johnson, 2009, p.16).

The professional development of teachers has been thought of as something that is done by others *for* or *to* teachers, and while post-secondary coursework, professional workshops, and educational seminars will most certainly continue to play an important role in the professional development of teachers, alternative professional development structures that allow for self-directed, collaborative, inquiry-based learning that is directly relevant to teachers' classrooms have begun to emerge (Johnson, 2009, p.95). Johnson (2009) lists Critical Friends Groups, Peer Coaching, Lesson Study, Cooperative Development, and Teacher Study Groups as models of inquiry-based approaches to professional development. As other models, CFGs also conceive of teacher professional development as collaborative and practitioner-driven, with an explicit focus on exploring and analysing the dynamic nature of student learning. These models have unique structural arrangements which create the potential for sustained dialogic mediation among teachers as they engage in goal-directed activity, and which provide assisted performance to those struggling through issues that are directly relevant to their classroom lives (Johnson, 2009, p.95).

The Sociocultural Theory of mind (SCT) is an appropriate theoretical lens for studying teacher development through CFG because it emphasizes the importance of mediated learning (Poehner, 2009). In other words, both SCT and CFG assume that learning is mediated by participation in social practices and therefore a good theoretical match.

Collaborative Teacher Development

Collaborative teacher development (CTD) is an increasingly common kind of teacher development found in a wide range of language teaching contexts. The idea of fostering collaborative professional communities in schools as means of improving teacher practice and thereby raising student achievement has gained currency in recent years. Research consistently points to collaboration as a model of professional development that substantially impacts instructional practice and improves student achievement outcomes (Şeker, 2007; Williams, 2010).

Teaching has no longer viewed as an occupation pursued in isolation from one's colleagues as Freeman (1998) described it as an "egg-box profession" in which each of us is kept separate from our fellow teachers. An important component of teacher development has been to overcome this isolation with collaborative endeavours both within and beyond the classroom (Johnston, 2009). Recent studies have acknowledged that teacher collaboration supports teachers' professional learning (McLaughlin & Talbert, 2006; Stoll & Louis, 2007; Doppenberg, den Brok & Bakx, 2012).

As Richards and Farrell (2005) stated, although much teacher development can occur through a teacher's own personal initiative, collaboration with others both enhances individual learning and serves the collective goals of an institution. Therefore, language teaching institutions support teachers working together in teams to maintain high professional standards, to pursue professional development by providing conditions where teachers collaborate and cooperate.

As Johnston (2009) defines CTD is any sustained and systematic investigation into teaching and learning in which a teacher voluntarily collaborates with others involved in the teaching process, and in which professional development is a prime purpose (p.242). There are two important features of CTD:

1. The teacher or teachers concerned must have, or share, control over the process-that is, this is not something one can "do to" teachers.

2. Professional development should not be seen merely as by-products of other development processes but needs to be built into them as a core component.

As the first feature suggests, teachers should voluntarily engage in shared decision making as they work toward a common goal. CTD arises from, and reinforces, a view of teacher learning as a fundamentally social process- in other words, that teachers can only learn professionally in sustained and meaningful ways when they are able to do so together (Johnston, 2009). Another point is that CTD supports a view of teachers both individually and as a community as producers, not just consumers, of knowledge and understanding about teaching (Freeman & Johnson, 1998; Johnston 2003, p.123-126). CTD arises from a belief that teaching can and should be a fundamentally collegial profession.

Erickson et al. (2005) also outline the features that represent collaborative model of professional development:

1- The school personnel must be involved at the very beginning of the project in negotiating the nature and the structure of the group.

2- The project must meet real and existing needs of all participants.

3- There is a need to sustain collaborative inquiry over a number of years.

4- There must be strong agreement from both school and teacher educators on the purposes and any underlying theoretical perspectives of the project. It is important that all participants hold or develop a similar perspective on learning.

5- The group must meet regularly (preferably once a week) and the chair of the meetings should maintain a close liaison with both school and university participants.

6- The group membership should be voluntary and flexible, yet overall group stability is an important characteristic.

7- The participants must be aware and sensitive to the different roles that are important to nurturing and maintenance functions of collaborative groups and recognize that each participant's role may change over time.

8- There must be some provision of resources for the group although these are primarily in the area of arranging sufficient and common blocks of time to attend regular meetings (p.794).

Collaboration by professional teaching faculty is one component of the popular Professional Learning Communities (PLC) school reform model. In this model, teachers are collaborative in their development of instruction, assessments, and examination of student work, seeking to determine essential learning outcomes and working to ascertain the best course of action for students who do not master essential learning outcomes or objectives. CTD can take different forms framed within various approaches to teacher development. Action research, narrative inquiry, cooperative development, exploratory practice, team teaching, teacher study groups, critical friends group, dialog journal writing, long-distance collaboration are some of these. The Critical Friends Group, as a professional learning community model, is applied in this study to maintain CTD. PLC will be dealt in the next section.

Professional Learning Communities

Although there is no universal definition of a professional learning community, it is commonly described as a group of teachers who are sharing and critically interrogating their practice in an on-going, reflective, collaborative, inclusive, learning-oriented, growth-promoting way (Stoll & Louis, 2007). Another recent definition is that a professional learning community is an inclusive group of people, motivated by a shared learning vision, who support and work with each other, finding ways, inside and outside their immediate community, to enquire on their practice and together learn new and better approaches that will enhance all pupils' learning (Stoll et al. 2006, p.5).

According to Clausen et.al (2009), the desire for a learning community format in schools is not a new one. For almost a hundred years, researcher/theorists from Dewey (1916) and Parsons (1959) to Fullan and Hargreaves (1991) have advocated that schools should look at themselves as social organizations (Clausen et.al, 2009, p.444). During the eighties, Rosenholtz (1989) brought teachers' workplace factors into the discussion of teaching quality, maintaining that teachers who felt supported in their own on-going learning and classroom practice were more committed and effective than those who did not receive such confirmation. McLaughlin and Talbert (1993) confirmed Rosenholtz's findings, suggesting that when teachers had opportunities for collaborative inquiry and the learning related to it, they were able to develop and share a body of wisdom gleaned from their experience.

The team-teaching movement, from the late 1950s and through the 1960s, makes a good starting point for a learning community. There have been many initiatives since then. As Crandall (personal communication, 11 July, 2012) has noted recently, referencing the recent research, educational institutions that align their performance goals to teachers' professional development through professional learning communities i.e. groups of teachers who meet regularly to plan, problem-solve, and learn together-will achieve positive outcomes.

The professional learning community model flows from the assumption that the core mission of formal education is not simply to ensure that students are taught but to ensure that they learn (DuFour, 2004). However, it is not easy in so many cases. The scenario DuFour represents is true for most of the schools. "A teacher teaches a unit to the best of his or her ability, but at the conclusion of the unit some students have not mastered the essential outcomes. On the one hand, the teacher would like to take the time to help those students. On the other hand, the teacher feels compelled to move forward to "cover" the course content. If the teacher uses instructional time to assist students who have not learned, the progress of students who have mastered the content will suffer, if the teacher pushes on with new concepts, the struggling students will fall farther behind" (DuFour, 2004, p.2). What typically happens in this situation is that the teacher is left at her discretion. When educators work together in a professional learning community, they can move beyond 'What are we expected to teach?' to 'How will we know when each student has learned?' by creating structures to promote a collaborative culture. They work together to analyse and improve their classroom practice. Teachers work in teams or groups, engaging in an on-going cycle of questions that promote learning. This process, in turn, leads to higher levels of student achievement.

DuFour, Eaker, and Dufour (2005), who are leaders of the PLC reform model, state:

> The use of PLCs is the best, least expensive, most professionally rewarding way to improve schools. In both education and industry, there has been a prolonged, collective cry for such collaborative communities for more than a generation now. Such communities hold out immense, unprecedented hope for schools and the improvement of teaching.

According to Snow-Gerono (2005) professional learning communities created opportunities for dialogue which made it safe to ask questions and work in a community where uncertainty was not only valued, but supported. She indicates that "good conversations" require "safety, trust, and care" as well as "common ground," "good content," and a sense of being voluntary.

Within collaborative groups which are considered as professional learning communities, Hindin et. al (2007) notes three key features that demonstrate promise in supporting teacher learning and changing classroom practice:

1. *Collaboration in the intellectual work of teaching.* Teachers engage over the school year in cycles of '...planning, enacting, and reflecting upon one's teaching'. Teachers become accepting of new practices as they try them out in a supported and safe context and observe the results in their own and each other's classrooms.

2. *A common orientation to teaching and learning.* Teachers work with a body of concepts and principles related to their content area and come to some shared understanding of those concepts and how to apply them.

3. *Sharing of expertise.* Teachers make available to one another their specialized content knowledge and 'pedagogical content knowledge,' instructional approaches for facilitating students' learning of the content.

'Critical Friends Group' is one of the collaborative learning communities that has been in action in the USA since 1994. In this study, it was used both as a tool to evaluate an INSET programmes and a professional learning community model for teacher professional development in a university context for the first time in Turkey.

INSET

Bolam (1986, as cited in Hopkins 1986) defines INSET as education and training activities engaged in by teachers and principals, following their initial professional certification, and intended primarily or exclusively to improve their professional knowledge, skills and attitudes in order that they can educate learners of all ages more effectively. Every teacher is a career-long student, and that portion of his education which follows in time, his initial certification and employment, is known as in-service teacher education. More recently, the Education Information Network in the European Union (EURYDICE) has defined in-service training as 'a variety of activities and practices in which teachers become involved in order to broaden their knowledge, improve their skills and assess and develop their professional approach' (Perron 1991, as cited in Bayrakçı 2009).

England (1998) emphasises the need for in-service teacher training and continuous education due to the change that takes place not only in education but also in the world. She argues that teacher development is a critical phenomenon by giving five reasons to explain its critical nature. Her very first reason is that the number of non-native speakers of English language is four times as many as the native speakers of English and this is the obvious sign of the significant role of English language teaching worldwide. Second reason is explained as the growth in the knowledge of English language teaching and learning. Third, she claims that the reason why many MA and certificate programs have added components of practical, real-world training as an effort to better prepare teachers for success following their academic programs. Fourth, England (1998) explains that teachers are the educators of others, therefore, "intrinsically want and need to participate in on-going development and change in their own professional lives." Obviously, teachers need to be supported in their efforts to develop themselves to change positively. Finally, England (1998) argues about support and guidance that teachers need to be provided for their professional improvement. She stresses the benefits of carefully designed professional in-service training as teachers are at the core of a quality ELT program. When teachers develop their skills in their professional application, then, the roles of teachers and students are believed to have evolved into partnerships in the learning process (Christison & Stoller, 1997).

Twenty-first century ELT practices require regular updates. Pre-service and in-service teacher training programs need to be coordinated continually and teachers should be provided on-going support to ensure change in the roles that they perform not only in their classrooms but also in the school environment. When teachers are provided professional support and guidance, they raise awareness on their professional applications and build confidence as a result they are empowered (Christison & Stoller, 1997) and they change. According to Güçeri (2005) this is a positive change which is reflected to their professional practice and empowered teachers commit themselves to more demanding tasks and play more significant role in their profession.

It is claimed that INSETs have confidence-building effect on teachers as INSETs help teachers not only raise awareness on pedagogic issues but also develop their personal qualities (Freeman, 1982; Güçeri, 2005; Şahin, 2006). While educational seminars, workshops, in-service courses play an important role in the professional development of L2 teachers, alternative professional development structures that allow for collaborative and inquiry-based learning have emerged. The Critical Friends Group is the model that supports collaborative learning and professional development. It can be used as an inquiry-based model for professional development or as a tool to evaluate any development strategies or structures as it was anticipated in this study.

INSET Models and Strategies

As mentioned earlier, INSET can address training or development needs. Training is characterised by objectives that are defined by a deficit in language, teaching skills or curricular knowledge; and they are defined by the gap between the teacher's current level of skill or knowledge and the level required by their role in the system (Roberts, 1998, p.221). The notion of development on INSET, on the other hand, implies objectives which allow for teachers' individual differences and which are determined by teachers' sense of their own learning needs and it also presupposes competence in basic skills and knowledge (Roberts, 1998). A teacher is a professional/ independent problem-solver, who takes responsibility for personal and professional development as aimed to be encouraged in this study.

INSET models appear to have numerous functions and draws upon many models and approaches. Roberts (1998) suggests four types of INSET according to how they are initiated and their purpose. These can be summarised as:

- Programmes in accordance with ITE
- Centrally determined programmes
- Locally determined content, with local control
- Determined with individual needs

O'Sullivan (2001), in her large scale study, summarises the strategies of effective INSET programmes, which helped her to devise the INSET strategies model. These are:

- School-based and school-focused programme
- Based on teachers' needs
- Related to classroom realities
- Opportunities to try out new skills
- Adequate supervision and follow-up
- Planned and formal in nature

However, to provide an effective INSET course requires considering broad issues related to teachers and teaching contexts. First, these courses need to value trainees' knowledge and experience, incorporate these in the act of learning and enhance the possibility of change by exploring context-specific constraints (Fishman et al., 2003). Moreover, the knowledge transmitted should not be far removed from the contexts of teachers, and situational factors affecting their classroom practices should be taken into account (Atay, 2008; Uysal, 2012). When professional development is planned and focused upon teachers' needs, it is likely to be more effective (Duncombe & Armour, 2004), and it leads to the development of in-service teaching programs that are feasible and within teachers' classroom realities. Finally, follow-up communication and guidance is taught to be inadequate in most INSET courses (Waters 2006, Bayrakci 2009, Uysal 2012), so adequate follow-up support and some sort of investigation after in-service programs are necessary in order to reveal the effectiveness of the courses.

In all INSET, as Roberts (1998) states, there is tension between the needs of the system and those of the individual, therefore the key task for the INSET provider is to address both and to negotiate between system wide and personal needs (p.223).

Butler, Lauscher, Jarvis-Selinger and Beckingham (2004:cited in Şeker, 2007) advocate more collaborative in- service professional development models against traditional models which include top-down approach to transfer knowledge to be translated into action. Behaviourist and cognitivist models are criticized as being expert driven and designed to convey procedural skills. However, for them, teaching is an intellectual activity that requires complex, contextualized decision-making. Teachers should be supported to work in collaborative groups to reconstruct their professional knowledge (Şeker, 2007). Butler et al. (2004) describe the system of such a group as follows:

> Groups of teachers and/or researchers work together locally, within schools, or peripherally, for example, in meeting separate from immediate practice, to develop new ways of teaching. Individually or collectively, teachers try out new ideas in classrooms and monitor the success of their efforts. They come together to review their instruction, talk about outcomes, and critically reflect on their teaching. Over time, within collaborative problem-solving groups, teachers develop a shared language for talking about teaching and co-construct knowledge within a discourse community (p.437).

Most INSET programmes require expert teachers to model and guide less experienced teachers, which in a sense is similar to the training scheme in behaviouristic approach. The input comes from outsider and the trainee is expected to internalize this outside input and establish new teaching behaviours accordingly (Hockly, 2000, cited in Şeker, 2007). However, unless teachers feel the need of the input or find it practical to apply in the classroom, familiarize the context with their own, or work in collaboration with their peers, these programmes may not help teachers' professional development.

The INSET Cycle

As Roberts (1998) states teacher learning takes time; it is gradual and cumulative; it requires a mix of experience, reflection, discussion and input. Therefore, INSET needs to be sustained over time; it should be seen as a process, not as a series of one-off events (p.231). The INSET cycle Roberts (1998) defines is in figure below:

Fig. 1 The INSET Cycle

Needs assessment and evaluation are of central importance. As mentioned before, the INSET should address both the needs of the system and the individuals of the system. Teachers need to be involved in the identification and articulation of their own training needs whenever possible (Rubin, 1978; cited in Roberts, 1998). A needs assessment should be seen by all parties as fair, open, and capable of reflecting the needs of all and not just of those in authority (Roberts, 1998).

These needs and objectives should be reviewed during the INSET programme because they evolve. According to Roberts (1998) once the INSET cycle is under way, the distinction between needs assessment and programme evaluation disappears. The major decisions in INSET evaluation is what to evaluate and why, who does it and how. An evaluation can improve teacher participation and ownership if real consultation and information sharing take place. Any INSET programme can provide teacher development when teachers are encouraged to reflect upon new ideas, activities and perspectives; when they have opportunities and support to put such ideas into practice, to reflect in and on their practices alongside a skilful critical friend; when teachers work collaboratively and get proper support to realise that new approaches work and are worthwhile. In recent decades, a great amount of literature has been generated to promote the transformation of staff development in the school system from a hierarchical, industrial model to one that advocates a more collegial, learning community (Clausen et.al, 2009). One of the teacher research communities is 'Critical Friends Group.

The Critical Friends Group (CFG)

CFG is 'a practitioner-driven study group that reflects the growing trend for site-based professional development in which practitioners behave as managers of their own learning' (Dunne & Honts 1998, as cited in Franzak, 2002, p. 260). A CFG is composed of peers where there is no 'hierarchy of expertise' and it must support a democratic, reflective, and collaborative community of learners (McKenzie & Carr-Reardon, 2003). The theoretical foundation for CFG is that teachers belonging to a group learn to collaborate by participating in professional development activities, and this participation leads to greater reflection on teaching techniques, which then supports a change in practice aimed at improving student achievement (Vo & Nguyen, 2009).

In 1994, the Annenberg Institute for School Reform designed a different approach to professional development, one that would be focused on the practitioner and on defining what would improve student learning. Since the summer of 2000, Critical Friends Groups training is coordinated by the National School Reform Faculty (NSRF), the professional development wing of the Annenberg Institute, at the Harmony Education Centre in Bloomington, Indiana.

CFG process acknowledges the complex art of teaching and provides structures for teachers to improve their teaching by giving and receiving feedback (Bambino, 2002). CFG allows its members to help each other to examine their own work and make changes whenever required (Bloom, 1999). When a colleague offers a critique of a person's work as a friend, this person acquires an important role to improve the practice. From a perspective of a Sociocultural Theory, learning occurs through social interaction rather than acquiring of skills needed to simply transmit knowledge. Thus, CFG is one such model of professional development that helps teachers to grow both individually and collectively.

The collaborative inquiry model presented by CFGs is grounded in the belief that teachers of all levels can mentor and support one another. Research examining pre-service teachers, novice teachers, and veteran teachers all indicates that CFGs promote the development of the professional self (Key, 2006). Moreover, research into CFG work has demonstrated that teachers seem to grow both individually and collectively when they are involved in such groups for professional development (Little, Gearhart, Curry, & Kafta, 2003; Curry, 2008; Nefstead, 2009). For example, Dunne, Nave and Lewis (2000) discovered that teachers involved in CFGs were more reflective about 'the connections among curriculum, assessment and pedagogy' which led to 'shift from teacher-centred to student-centred instruction' (p.10). Teachers were also more likely to change their method of instruction if students were not succeeding, felt more confident with the implementation of new methods, and were able to look at their classroom practice from a variety of perspectives. As with other collaborative models of teacher professional development, critical friends groups change the look and feel of traditional professional development programs.

The Critical Friends Group Model

A CFG was defined on the National School Reform Faculty website (NSRF, 2011) as "a professional learning community consisting of approximately eight to twelve educators who come together voluntarily at least once a month for about two hours. Group members are committed to improving their practice through collaborative learning". According to NSRF (2011), Critical Friends Groups are designed to

- Create a professional learning community,
- Make teaching practice explicit and public by "talking about teaching",
- Help people involved in schools to work collaboratively in democratic, reflective communities,
- Establish a foundation for sustained professional development based on a spirit of inquiry,

- Provide a context to understand our work with students, our relationships with peers, and our thoughts, assumptions, and beliefs about teaching and learning,
- Help educators help each other turn theories into practice and standards into actual student learning,
- Improve teaching and learning.

CFG members bring to the table their students' work, lesson plans and units, case studies of students, classroom dilemmas, peer observation evidence, and prospective texts. Using structures called protocols to guide their discussion, CFG members help each other "tune" their teaching by analysing and critiquing artifacts, observations and issues pertaining to their practice (CES, 2008). At the NSRF Research forum in January 2007, Ross Peterson-Veatch presented a visual illustration that depicted the "beliefs, values, and assumptions; process; culture or conditions; and outcome" of the CFG model (Peterson-Veatch, 2007). Figure 2 summarizes the CFG model and its outcomes.

Fig.2 CFGs and Transformation

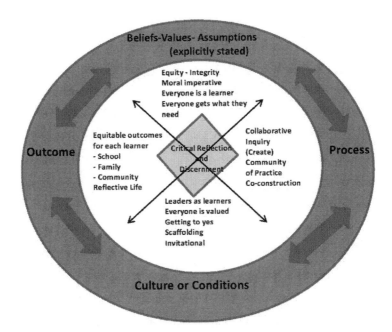

On-going professional development is one way for teachers to continue to renew themselves in their practice. Dedicated teachers learn throughout their careers, actively participating in a culture where they learn more about the content they teach and about the instructional and assessment practices they use with that content. To change their practice, teachers must go through a regular process of self-analysis, inquiry, and reflection.

Each CFG meets for at least two hours, once or twice a month with a trained coach or facilitator. Over the course of a school year, this can add up to 18-30 hours of teacher development. Many Coalition Schools have multiple CFGs, and typically, the groups broaden their perspective and connections with others through partnerships and regional meetings with CFG's from other schools (CES, 2008).

The common characteristics of CFGs, according to Dunne and Honts (1998), are uninterrupted time for collegiality, reflective practice and time for critical thinking. Collegiality is one of the key words in the current literature on school reform; however, there is a huge gap between knowing what is important, to whom this would be important and actually working together in a collegial manner. CFG model enables teachers to create a time for collegiality because this model contrasts with traditional methods of professional development, in which outside experts arrive at school to examine their innards and inject them with whatever ready-made remedies they think best. Moreover, the heart of CFG model is creating a community of learners that work from a shared set of values and beliefs and willing to question those beliefs and assumptions in a safe environment where no one judges one another. Reflective comments from participants demonstrate that there are thirty-year veterans who recognize for the first time in their careers not only do they need change, but also how to change to benefit the learner of today (Baron, 2005; cited in Kelley, 2007).

Reflective practice is viewed as a means by which practitioners can develop a greater level of self-awareness about the nature and impact of their performance, an awareness that creates opportunities for professional growth and development (Osterman & Kottkamp, 1993). CFG model simply creates the environment for reflection with a group of colleagues, not in isolation. To work in a CFG gives an opportunity to listen to co-workers and learn from them and allows evaluating one's teaching style. Armstrong (2003) asserts that the CFGs she studied did partially support teacher's reflection on teaching practice. Group members became more aware of their practice and of their need to grow. Peer observations, when conducted, provided opportunities for problem posing while tuning protocols and observations both provide evidence of inquiry into practice.

The Critical Friends Group Protocols

According to NSFR, the word "protocol" has taken on a more specific meaning in education in recent years. In the context of educators working to improve their practice, a protocol is a structured process or set of guidelines to promote meaningful and efficient communication and learning. Gene Thompson-Grove, co-director of the national CFG project, writes, "[protocols] permit a certain kind of conversation to occur -often a kind of conversation which people are not in the habit of having. Protocols are vehicles for building the skills and culture necessary for collaborative work. Thus, using protocols often allows groups to build trust by actually doing substantive work together."

From another point of view, protocols are the methods of analysis used to objectively critique assignments in order to improve teaching techniques and student learning. In order to maintain a professional, objective, and productive method of analysing student work, it is important to use a protocol that meets the needs of your CFG.

Despite the unique nature of CFG, they have similar implications to other professional development models that also involve teacher discourse, such as teacher support groups and peer coaching. CFGs, like these two other collaborative models of professional development, provide teachers with opportunities to collaborate with other teachers in a structured and trusting environment. Unlike other models, CFGs are structured around specific protocols, procedural steps and guidelines, which are both time and topic driven and drive the teacher to delve deeper into the dilemma. Allen and Blythe (2004) mentioned that these protocols guide conversations to look beyond the surface of a "problem" to the many layers that lie beneath it. Protocols, therefore, "promote among colleagues both exploration of important areas of teaching and learning as well as sustained collaborative inquiry into particular questions about teaching and learning (p.11)".

The protocols also regulate who speaks, and when and how they do so, while acknowledging that what the group notices or says is spontaneous and therefore hard to predict (Poehner, 2009). Each protocol allows time for the following: the presenter to provide the team with the context (background information) for the work; individual and group analyses after closely examining the work; asking both clarifying (fact) and probing (to expand thinking) questions to fully understand the problem; hearing the presenter's reflections on the process (p.11).

Many protocols involve one or a small group of presenting educators and another small group of "consulting" educators. The Tuning Protocol was one of the first, and that term is sometimes used as a generic term for many similar protocols. Since its trial run in 1992, the Tuning Protocol has been widely used and adapted for professional development purpose. The overview of this protocol can give a clearer idea about how the protocols work: To take part in the Tuning Protocol, educators bring samples of either own work or their students' work on paper and, whenever possible, on video, as well as some of the materials they have created to support student performance, such as assignment descriptions and scoring rubrics. In a circle of about six to ten "critical friends" (usually other educators), a facilitator guides the group through the process and keeps time. The presenting educator, or team of educators, describes the context for the student work (the task or project) - uninterrupted by questions or comments from participants. Often the presenter begins with a focusing question or area about which she would especially welcome feedback, for example, "Are you seeing evidence of persuasive writing in the students' work?" Participants have time to examine the student work and ask clarifying questions. Then, with the presenter listening but silent, participants offer warm and cool feedback - both supportive and challenging. Presenters often frame their feedback as a question, for example, "How might the project be different if students chose their research topics?" After this feedback is offered, the presenter has the opportunity, again uninterrupted, to reflect on the feedback and address any comments or questions she chooses. Time is reserved for debriefing the experience. Table 5 in Chapter 3 summarizes the Tuning Protocol. Protocols are sometimes modified by their users, but it is highly recommended that users try them exactly as they are written several times before making modifications. The protocols used in this study will be presented in much greater detail in the following chapter.

As seen in the literature presented, teachers are more likely to change their classroom practice when they are provided with a safe and nurturing environment where they can share both dilemmas and positive teaching stories than when they are mandated to attend training programs in which externals authorities address general pedagogical issues. It can also be argued that the protocols that are utilized in Critical Friends Group sessions are the tools that help teachers mediate their understanding of how they construct a problem they are encountering and create the environment to solve and move on towards more satisfying teaching and learning practices.

Chapter 2   Research Design and Methodology

Research Method and Overall Research Design

This research study is designed as a qualitative case study, aiming to explore the impact of in-service teacher training programme on teachers' professional development, and the implementation of Critical Friends Group as a tool both to evaluate the programme and to support professional teacher development. The qualitative research is the methodology preferred as it enables the researcher to have an in-depth look at the issue by communicating to the individual teachers and school administrators concerned one to one basis so that the answers to how they perceived the roles, how they acted or how things were done could be identified (Frankeal & Wallen, 2000). Qualitative research is not simple to define as researchers have their own definitions and use distinct terms to refer to it. 'Descriptive research', 'naturalistic methods', 'field methods', 'qualitative inquiry', 'inductive research' are among the others that have been used synonymously. Regardless of what term is employed, qualitative research remains to be the umbrella term and interpreted as referring to "the meanings, concepts, definitions, characteristics, metaphors, symbols, descriptions of things" (Berg, 1989:2).

Qualitative inquiry has long been effectively used by social sciences, particularly of anthropology, history, sociology and, political sciences. Qualitative research begins with the belief that each social setting is unique unto itself and its inhabitants. This research paradigm operates with the assumption that "objects, pictures, or detailed descriptions cannot be reduced to numbers without distorting the essence of the social meanings they represent," thus, this model is well suited for the unique contexts the public school researcher encounters (Hatch, 2002, p.9). Hatch (2002) considers it a hallmark of high quality qualitative research that researchers work from extended periods of engagement within the research context and with the research participants. This extended engagement allows the researcher to gain intimate knowledge of the participants and their interactions with each other and their contexts, making the assembly of knowledge from the data collection process more succinct, with the researcher possessing a deeper understanding of the participants and context about which they write. Hatch (2002) states, "I understand the practicalities of doing research, especially doctoral dissertation research, but overall, qualitative researchers are not spending enough time being intensely engaged in the settings they are studying" (p. 8). Table 3 shows the characteristics of qualitative research from three different perspectives. According to Creswell (2007), it is necessary for the qualitative researcher to consider his or her own paradigms and worldviews as these will act as information filters that inform the researcher's interpretations of data in the writing of qualitative research.

Table 3 Characteristics of Qualitative Research

Characteristics	LeCompte & Schensul (1999)	Marshall &Rossman (2006)	Hatch (2002)
Natural setting, a source of data for close interaction	Yes	Yes	Yes
Researcher as a key Instrument of data collection			Yes
Multiple data sources in words or images	Yes	Yes	Yes
Analysis of data inductively, recursively, interactively	Yes	Yes	Yes
Focus on participants' perspectives, their meanings, their subjective views	Yes		Yes
Framing of human behaviour and belief within a socio-political/ historical context or through a cultural lens	Yes		
Emergent rather than tightly prefigured design		Yes	Yes
Fundamentally interpretive inquiry—researcher reflects on her or his role, the role of the reader, and the role of the participants shaping the study		Yes	
Holistic view of social phenomena		Yes	Yes

(Creswell, 2007, p.38)

The qualitative case study is an approach to research that facilitates exploration of a phenomenon within its context using a variety of data sources. This ensures that the issue is not explored through one lens, but rather a variety of lenses which allows for multiple facets of the phenomenon to be revealed and understood (Baxter & Jack, 2008; 544). According to Merriem (1990, as cited in Nefstead 2009), "case study, which is known to be a form of descriptive, non-experimental research, is inductive in nature and can test or build theory. Most case studies in education are qualitative and 'hypothesis-generating', rather than quantitative and 'hypothesis-testing studies' (p. 8).

"The case study research method is an empirical inquiry that investigates a contemporary phenomenon with its real-life context; when the boundaries between phenomenon and context are not clearly evident; and in which multiple sources of evidence are used" (Yin, 1994). In a qualitative study the observations and analyses are filtered through the senses of the researcher as the primary instrument of data collection and analysis. Denzin and Lincoln (2000) described the qualitative researcher as a "quilt maker" who "stitches, edits, and puts slices of reality together" (p.5). Creswell (2005, p.450) stated that 'for a case study, the focus is on developing an in-depth understanding of a case, such as an event, activity, or a process. In education, this often includes the study of an individual or several individuals, such as students or teachers.' Case-study researchers may focus on a program, event, or activity involving individuals rather than a group. Generally, the activities of the group are more focused than identifying shared patterns of behaviour exhibited by the group. According to Creswell (2005), case study researchers focus on an in-depth exploration of the actual 'case'. Therefore, a case study's design corresponded with the purpose of this research which was to evaluate the impact of an INSET programme and whether CFG played any role in teachers' professional development. Each 'Critical Friend' was considered as a case in the study and case study approach has been employed while evaluating the CFG participants' perceptions.

Creswell illustrated the procedures for developing a case study design in educational research as shown in Table 4. Similar procedures were followed while conducting this study.

Table 4 Procedure for a Case Study

Procedures for Conducting a Case Study Procedures	Case Study
Identify the intent, the appropriate design, and how intent relates to the research problem	The problem relates to developing an in-depth understanding of a "case" or bounded system. The problem relates to understanding an event, activity, process, or one or more individuals. Identify the type of "case" such as intrinsic, instrumental, or collective.
Discuss how researcher plans to receive approval and gain access to study sites and participants.	Receive approval from instructional review board. Locate a research site using purposeful sampling procedures. Identify how many cases the researcher plans to study. Identify a gatekeeper to provide access. Guarantee provisions for respecting the site.
Collect appropriate data emphasizing time in the field, multiple sources of information, and collaboration.	Collect extensive data using multiple forms of data collection (Observation, interviews, documents, audio-visual materials).
Analyse and interpret the data within a design.	Read through data to develop an overall understanding of it. Describe the case(s) in detail and establish a context for it. Develop issues or themes about the case(s). If more than one case is studied, consider a within-case analysis followed by a cross-case analysis.

This study began with the belief that 'continuing professional development' which can be addressed by INSET and followed by CFG is essential for the instructors in this research context. The creation of collegial professional learning environment supports and fosters teaching and learning. The instructors at the School of Mersin University had never been participated in any in-service programme implemented by the institution, designed for their needs. The survey conducted at the very beginning of the study revealed the instructors' willingness and desire to such programmes. They also expressed in what areas they need in-service training. The challenge of this research was to design the context of the training according to the teachers' needs. The proposed five-day-INSET-programme was changed into a once-a-month-seminar-programme by the director of the School. The process of developing a professional learning community through the implementation of a CFG was supported by the volunteer instructors and the protocols were successfully followed. The academic year

2010 through 2011 was the time frame for the study of the CFG. In the second phase, INSET seminars were followed by CFG meetings. Protocols were used to evaluate the process.

"The vision of practice that underlies the nation's reform agenda requires most teachers to rethink their own practice, to construct new classroom roles and expectations about student outcomes, and to teach in ways they have never taught before" (Darling-Hammond & McLaughlin, 1995). To this end, this research was designed to create a professional learning community where teachers taught about their practice while discussing and observing their friends. Development-based in-service teacher training programme sessions were also evaluated.

Conceptual and Theoretical Frameworks Underpinning CFG

The conceptual construct of CFG that is utilized in this dissertation has been presented in the literature review in Chapter 1. To recap, the concept of CFG was created at the Annenberg Institute for School Reform (AISR) in 1994. Educators from three organizations, the Coalition of Essential Schools (CES), the AISR, and National School Reform Faculty (NSRF), participated in the 1994 design of CFG. This teacher professional development programme is collaborative and practitioner-driven. CFG is not designed as an evaluative tool for teachers; it is uninterrupted time for collegiality, reflective practice and time for critical thinking.

All conversations within CFGs are structured around protocols that are both time and topic driven. They were designed to enable teachers to analyse and reflect on different aspects of teaching practice and learning process, or external resources such as textbooks, supplementary materials, and videos. Protocols are, therefore, designed to look at issues by raising open-ended questions that emerge from work or seeking solutions to specific problems that exist.

The CFG process begins with the session facilitator, the researcher in this dissertation, collaboratively planning the CFG meeting. During the group meeting, the facilitator uses the format of the protocol to guide the discussions and to keep it focused. Although these protocols are structured, they are not completely rigid; they can be slightly altered to fit the group's needs and learning goals. The participants are expected to be thoughtful as they engage in critical and positive discourse in order to understand the situation from a variety of perspectives. No member is superior to the other; there is no hierarchy between the participants. Thoughtful discussion was one element of good professional development, a goal of CFGs. Conversation centred on investigating a teacher's practice will change and hopefully enhance teacher practice in order to improve student learning. At the end of the presentation, the group discusses the effectiveness of the protocol. As part of their CFG work, teachers collect and reflect on evidence from their practice, focusing on progress toward shared standards or exploring a particular question about learning and teaching.

The theoretical roots of communities of learners can be traced back to Russian psychologist Lev Vygotksy's concept of the zone of proximal development (1978, p.86). Although Vygotsky is referring to the learning and development of children, this can be transferred to the development of adults in new learning situations. Lave and Wenger continued with Vygotsky's idea of social constructivism and emphasized the learning of the whole individual in the learning community. They stated:

> Activities, tasks, functions, and understanding do not exist in isolation; they are part of a broader system of relations in which they have meaning. These systems of relations arise out of and are reproduced and developed within social communities, which are in part systems of relations among persons. (Lave & Wenger, 1991, p.53)

Constructivist learning theorist Gordon Wells (2000) built on the social constructivist theories of Lave and Wenger (1991) and Vygotsky (1978) with the following assertion:

> Teacher colleagues constitute co-participants in the community of inquiry, both teachers in the same school and kindred spirits in other institutions, both school and university. In such professional communities of inquiry, some of the most productive transformations of schooling are being carried out, often using a social constructivist framework to assist them (p.66).

Taking up a sociocultural perspective on L2 teacher education refocuses our orientation toward the professional development of L2 teachers (Johnson, 2009). As for Johnson, it shifts the focus of attention onto teachers as learners of L2 teaching and it highlights the socially situated nature of teacher learning (p.16). Several studies have supported Vygotsky's claim that mediation enables people to achieve more than they would be able to do alone (Gindis, 2003, Miller 2003, Pavlenko & Lantolf, 2000).

While CFG promotes collaborative work among participant teachers, it is difficult to ascertain how the CFG sessions actually lead to changes in how teachers think about and approach their current and future practices. This is the crux of the argument that CFGs are an effective model of teacher professional development. One of the central tenets of Sociocultural Theory is learning through mediated activity and, therefore, CFG is believed to be the model that can support teacher development while evaluating the INSET programme teachers go through.

In this study, CFG model was used to evaluate not the teachers but the impact of the INSET programme on teachers. Three protocols were applied during the meetings in the first part of the study. Then, the INSET took place. CFG meetings were arranged after the seminars and participant teachers were asked to discuss about what they got out of the presentations. In this part of the study, four protocols guided the conversations. The protocols and the outline of the CFG study will be presented next.

Protocols and CFG Meetings

According to NSRF, a protocol consists of agreed upon guidelines for a conversation. This type of structure permits much focused conversations to occur. Protocols set rules for who speaks, when, and about what, in essence framing the discourse. Protocols are used for looking at student and adult work, giving and receiving feedback, solving problems or dilemmas, observing classrooms or peers, to push thinking on a given issue and to structure a discussion around a text. One of the central purposes of CFG was to "make teaching practice explicit and public by 'talking about teaching' and providing a context to understand our work with students." Protocols are the tools that serve for this purpose.

Besides evaluating the impact of the INSET, the study also focused on the effects of the CFG model on teachers' professional development. To this end, three protocols were used at the beginning of the study. Table 3 presents the first protocol named 'Tuning Protocol'. The "Tuning Protocol" was developed by David Allen and Joe McDonald at the Coalition of Essential Schools primarily for use in looking closely at student exhibitions (Cushman, 1996). A "Tuning Protocol" was often used to keep the group meeting focused and within a specific time limit.

Table 5 Tuning Protocol: A Process for Reflection on Teacher and Student Work

I. Introduction	10 minutes	Facilitator briefly introduces protocol goals, norms, and agenda. Participants briefly introduce themselves.
II. Teacher Presentation	20 minutes	Presenter describes the context for student work (its vision, coaching, scoring rubric, etc.) and presents samples of student work (such as photo-copied pieces of written work or video tapes of an exhibition).
III. Clarifying Questions	15 minutes maximum	Facilitator judges if questions more properly belong as warm or cool feedback than as clarifiers.
IV. Pause to reflect on warm and cool feedback	2-3 minutes maximum	Participants make note of "warm," supportive feedback and 'cool," more distanced comments (generally no more than one of each).
V. Warm and Cool Feedback	15 minutes	Participants among themselves share responses to the work and its context; teacher-presenter is silent. Facilitator may lend focus by reminding participants of an area of emphasis supplied by teacher-presenter.
VI. Reflection/ Response	15 minutes	Teacher-presenter reflects on and responds to those comments or questions he or she chooses to. Participants are silent. Facilitator may clarify or lend focus.
VII. Debrief	10 minutes	Beginning with the teacher-presenter ("How did the protocol experience compare with what you expected?"), the group discusses any frustrations, misunderstandings, or positive reactions participants have experienced. More general discussion of the tuning protocol may develop.

Note. From NSRF, 2008, The Harmony Education Centre, Bloomington, IN. http://www.nsrfharmony.org.

The second protocol was the Charrette Protocol. It is a problem solving type of protocol which opens with the presenter asking a question about a specific dilemma. Participants then ask probing questions and discuss the problem among themselves, while the presenter takes notes until the discussion is finished, at which point the presenter shares what he or she heard that was useful or important for his or her dilemma (Appendix B). The last was the protocol 'The Final Word'. The purpose of this discussion format is to give each participant in the group to have their ideas, understandings, and perspectives enhanced by hearing from others. To this end, the group read an article on 'Multiple Intelligence' and tried to explore the article. Table 6 demonstrates the protocol guidelines.

Table 6 The Final Word

Purpose:	To explore the article, clarify our thoughts, expand our perspectives, and build on each other's thinking.
Key to facilitation:	Monitor timing and avoid dialogue.
Form:	Sit in a circle. Four people in a group work best.
Four rounds will occur:	Each round takes approximately seven minutes. Each round will begin with one person followed by the other three.
Three minutes:	The first person begins by reading what "struck them the most" from the text. One thought or quote.
One minutes per person:	Proceed around the circle each person responds briefly.
One minute:	The person that began then has the "final word" to respond to what has been said.
One minute:	The next person in the circle then begins by sharing what struck them
Role of facilitator:	To keep it moving, keep it clear and directed to the article, make connections and keep time so everyone gets an opportunity to speak.
Role of facilitator:	Debrief the process after group has finished.

Note. From NSRF, 2008, The Harmony Education Center, Bloomington, IN. http://www.nsrfharmony.org.

The second phase of the study was when the INSET programme was realized. Four more protocols were used during the CFG meetings. These were Classroom Evaluation: Success Analysis Protocol, Classroom Atmosphere and Examining Student Work: A Constructivist Protocol, Effective Use of Technology in the Classroom: Constructivist Tuning Protocol, Motivation: Dilemmas Protocol. In Table 7, a sample schedule of the CFG meetings and activities of 2010 Fall Term is presented. During some meetings, participants did not use any protocol. They were aimed for more professional development of the teachers. For each meeting, teachers were asked to write evaluation notes on their journals with the guided questions below:

Interpretation: What was significant to you? Why?

What inferences can you make about what the speaker said or why he said it that way?

Application: How might I use this in my classroom or with my Critical Friends Group? What would I do differently?

Table 7 Schedule of the CFG meetings and the activities

CFG #	Subject of Meetings	Time & Location
1	Classroom Evaluation ('Success Analysis Protocol')	Wednesdays, 15:00 to 16:00 Room 406
2	Classroom Atmosphere/Cooperative Learning ('Examining Student Work: A Constructivist Protocol')	Wednesdays, 15:00 to 16:00 Room 406
3	Dimensions of Learning / Integrated Skills (The focus-framing question exercise)	Wednesdays, 15:00 to 16:00 Room 406
4	Assessment (Alternative ways of Assessment)	Wednesdays, 15:00 to 16:00 Room 406
5	Peer Observations (Learning from classroom visits- Observation Protocol)	Wednesdays, 15:00 to 16:00 Room 406
6	Effective Use of Technology in the Classroom	Wednesdays, 15:00 to 16:00 Room 406
7	Motivation ('Constructivist Tuning Protocol')	Wednesdays, 15:00 to 16:00 Room 406
8	Materials Development, Culture in the Course-books	Wednesdays, 15:00 to 16:00 Room 406

The Context, Participants and the INSET Needs Analysis

The study was conducted at Mersin University, the School of Foreign Languages. The School has been running compulsory preparatory English courses for the students of some departments and faculties, and compulsory joint English courses for the first year students of other faculties and schools since 2002. At present, the School includes 48 instructors teaching preparatory and joint English courses, and 31 instructors are assigned to work within some faculties and schools. Among them, 8 instructors teach German and French in different faculties.

The School aims to provide the students whose level of English is below proficiency level with basic language skills so that they can pursue their undergraduate and graduate studies at the university. To achieve this aim, the department runs a two-semester intensive program placing emphasis on use of English, reading, writing, listening and speaking. Students are placed into groups according to their levels of English and have 22 or 26 class hours per week all through the academic year.

Joint English courses are given to first year students whose departments do not require any preparatory English course. At the beginning of the academic year, the students are given an exam in order to be exempted from this course. Those who could not get satisfactory grade take English course for 4 hours a week through two semesters.

The INSET programme was planned to be conducted for the School, including two assistant directors and the director. Before the INSET, a needs analysis was applied. Total number of participants was 36. The analysis was done twice, one by the researcher through written survey (Appendix C) and the other by the INSET Unit of the School, which the researcher was part of, through online. The number of survey participants showed similarity, 38 for the written, and 36 for the online. The Table 7 shows the gender, year of experience and current educational qualifications of the participants who joined the survey.

Table 8 The gender, year of experience and current educational qualifications of the participant instructors

Gender	Female % 86	Male % 14	
Year of Experience	Below 10 years % 31	Above 10 years % 69	
Current Education Qualifications	BA % 55	MA % 42	PhD % 3

The participants who had experience in other institutions, including Ministry of Education, mentioned that they had participated in some in-service training activities, but those who had a fresh start in Mersin University, the School of Foreign Languages have not had the chance to be a part of such programmes. Considering this need, the instructors were asked whether they need any INSET programme designed for the school and 82% of the participants would like to join an INSET programme especially designed in accordance with their needs. Main issues raised in the written survey were about improving foreign language skills, mainly speaking; supporting student motivation for learning, promoting use of computer and informative techniques and introducing new methods and forms of teaching. Testing language skills and supporting teacher motivation were the other two points which deserved attention. Figure 3 illustrates the outcomes of the written survey.

The teachers were also asked the direction of activities they believed to be prior in their school. General belief was that improving quality of education would be possible by supporting teacher development and motivation. Introducing new forms of teaching and techniques suitable for the needs of current students were highly welcomed. As for the expectations of the participants, they believed that the INSET could improve and renovate their existing knowledge, inform them about educational innovations, help them reflect on their teaching practices and provide opportunities to exchange experience and views. Consequently, the instructors believed that students' motivation and knowledge would improve.

Figure 3 The areas to be considered for the INSET programme

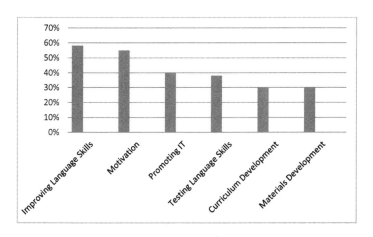

The online survey was conducted following the written one. Similar results came out from this survey as well. Figure 4 shows the areas in which the participants would like and expect to have training. These 10 subjects were considered to be extremely important for the instructors to be improved.

Figure 4 The subjects considered to have a priority in the INSET programme

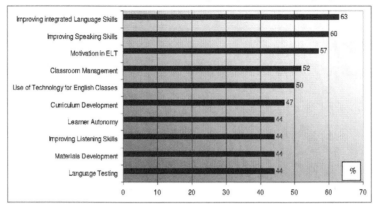

The INSET programme was tried to be designed according to the needs analysis by the researcher. The director of the School decided the final INSET subjects and the participant scholars. The visiting professors were informed beforehand about the subject matters that the instructors would like to be informed.

CFG Participant Selection

At the beginning of the study, the instructors at the school were given a short presentation about CFG (Appendix D) and the outline of the research was presented. It was clearly stated that CFG is not meant to be an evaluative tool, but rather a means for teachers to direct their own learning and reflection. The volunteers were asked to join the study. The sample selected for this study was 10 out of 36 instructors at Mersin University School of English. Due to some excuses, such as moving to another city, giving birth to a child, the Critical Friends remained 6. The consent form which explains the purpose, benefits, risks and confidentiality of the study was signed by each participant (Appendix E). The instructors ranged in teaching experience from novice teachers with three year experience to veteran teachers with over 15 years of experience. Two instructors had a master's degree. All instructors were female. They were new to CFG process. The group leader was the researcher herself for each meeting; however, the critical friends directed and created their own learning as they brought issues to be discussed collaboratively. The group members, therefore, were provided with opportunities to reflect beyond surface classroom issues to deep dilemmas that are at the root of their practice.

The original designers of the CFG envisioned a group of six to eight teacher volunteers participating in a group meeting for one to two hours per month in a school culture focused on student learning. Ideally, teachers would be asked to devote two hours per month for two years for group meetings. In this study, CFG meetings were held approximately twice a month over the course of two academic years. There were a few months only one meeting was held. Each meeting was approximately 50 minutes in duration, necessitating the adjustment of the suggested protocol times.

The CFG design encourages teacher-driven discussion. The study participants were asked to make decisions regarding group activities. During meetings, the teachers decided on various topics including time management, classroom management, assessment, student writing, teacher pedagogy, and peer observation. Agenda items of each meeting were noted down (Appendix F), the sessions were recorded and participants were asked to keep journals. All conversations within CFG are structured around specific protocols (procedural steps and guidelines). The protocols were both taken from NSRF website and designed by the researcher for the needs of the group. Although protocols may differ in their format and the way in which they are used, they share common elements; sharing question and dilemma, giving and receiving feedback, inviting questions from the participants. The participants brought some issues to the meetings to be discussed. Observation Protocol is in Appendix G.

The INSET Programme

Numerous studies have been conducted to evaluate the impact of in-service teacher training programs. The focus has been either on the input, that is, the course content or the output, that is, how the program affects the teaching of its participants. The long and short term benefits of professionally designed INSETs in teacher learning have also been emphasized by scholars. The researcher aimed to organize a five-day INSET program at the beginning of the study after taking the director's consent. However, due to unexpected institutional constraints, the programme was expanded through three academic terms. Approximately one meeting in a month was organized through two academic terms. All the instructors participated to the seminars and the workshops were given by the professors from different faculties and by two instructors from the school, one being the researcher herself. The topics were decided by the director of the school, considering the needs analysis. The seminars majored on motivation, bilingualism, classroom management, and teacher development. Table 9 shows the INSET programme organized by the institution.

Improving language skills and using technology were the subjects discussed mainly in the meetings. Hence, the researcher allocated time during the CF meetings to discuss the issues elaborately. For example, after the session on motivation, the group first evaluated the seminar, talked about the topics they found important and deserved attention, and then by using "Dilemmas" protocol each participant raised an issue that she had difficulty in. Other members of the group listened, made comments, and suggested ways to overcome the problem. Sharing the dilemmas the teachers had revealed different aspects of teacher practice and created an atmosphere where colleagues became consultants of their friends.

After each INSET seminar, all the participants of the school were asked to evaluate the session both by the institution in a written format and by the researcher orally. After two academic terms, the general evaluation was performed via interviews by the researcher. The results will be discussed in the next chapter. CFG members wrote their reflections after each INSET session in their diaries.

Table 9 INSET Seminars

Evaluating foreign languages teaching in Turkey	Prof. Dr. Mehmet Gündoğdu
Revealing students' and teachers' attitudes by metaphors: Time to motivate	Inst. Nafiye Çiğdem Aktekin
Training and competence in materials development	Inst. Selvin Güven
Communication in classroom	Prof. Dr. Ünsal Yetim
The priorities in basic language skills in foreign language teaching	Assist. Prof. Aytekin Keskin
Three Particularly Problematic Grammar Issues For English Language Learners	Prof. Dr. Keith Folse (Video presentation)
Making headway to success	Elna Coetzer (OUP Trainer)

Data Collection

The data came from the questionnaire and interviews, the meeting transcripts, the journals the teachers kept and the researcher's notes.

Audio-Recording of CFG Meetings and Protocols

CFGs made use of protocols that guide discussion during group meetings to promote reflective thinking. A protocol, as defined by the NSRF, was an agreed-upon guideline that facilitates focused conversation and review of both student and adult work, guides the giving and receiving of feedback, assists in solving problems or dilemmas, guides classroom or peer observations, encourages cognitive thinking on any given issue, and structures discussion surrounding professional literature. The assumption was that reflecting resulting from protocol-guided discussion promoted positive change in teaching practices and thus improved student learning.

The initial purpose of the CFG meetings was to elicit participants' impressions of and reflections on particular INSET sessions. However, CFG meetings created an environment for the teachers' professional development. During the meetings, protocols provided the participating teachers an opportunity to read and discuss professional literature, to review student data, to provide feedback on classroom planning, to guide debriefing following peer observation, and to review student work. Each protocol provided CFG members with guidelines for discussions through a series of steps in which insights from the classrooms, student performance, and institutional constraints were often the cornerstones. Data collection began with tape recording the CFG sessions. In total, 12 hours of the resulting eight CFG meetings were transcribed.

After each INSET session, non-CFG participants were also interviewed. A total of 40 semi-structured interviews with a total of 10 teachers were conducted. Interviews lasted from 10 to 20 minutes. The interviews focused on what the teachers thought about the workshop or the lecture and if the INSET session met their needs in terms of professional development.

Journals

A journal is a teacher's or a student teacher's written response to teaching events (Richard and Lockhart, 1994), and it serves two purposes:

      1- Events and ideas are recorded for the purpose of later reflection and

      2- The process of writing itself helps trigger insights about teaching. Writing in this sense serves as a discovery process (p.7).

The CFG participants were given some questions at the beginning of the study to reflect what they initially perceive from the process of CFG. Participants kept reflective journals that have detailed their experiences in each group session as part of their involvement as well as the answers of these reflective questions. These questions were reassembled at the end of the study in order to have the final perceptions of the participants about CFG. The evaluation of the INSET sessions was also noted in these journals. Since 'how to keep the journal' was discussed at the beginning of the study, teachers tried to keep their journals under three headings; reflections from the meetings, from the class and from the INSET (Appendix H).

The pre-evaluation questions were as follows:

1. What are your initial perceptions in terms of your definition of a Critical Friends Group?

2. How do you think the use of Critical Friends Group may change your perceptions of your school, classroom and colleagues?

3. What changes in your instructional strategies will occur as a result of your participation in CFG?

Questionnaires and Interviews

To find the answer for the first two research questions of the study, which are "What are the attitudes and expectations of Turkish EFL teachers at Foreign Languages School of Mersin University concerning the effects of development-based INSET programme?" and "In what areas do the teachers think they need training and development?", a questionnaire was conducted. The initial questionnaire was applied by the researcher to all the staff of the School in order to reveal the areas on which teachers thought they need to develop. The direction of the activities and the expectation

55

concerning the effects of the INSET were also inquired. After the programme, the researcher asked the instructors who did not participate in CFG whether their expectations were fulfilled or not. Their responses helped the researcher to answer the last research question of the study.

The Unit which was founded by the administration to organize the INSET activities in the School also administered an online questionnaire aiming at analysing the needs of teachers for the INSET. Semi-structured interviews were also organized in the School to determine the attitudes and expectations of the teachers.

Researcher's Notes

Each CFG session is run by a trained CFG coach from the school. The coach typically facilitates one of several time managed protocols for examining a dilemma or piece of work brought to the group by one of its members. The coach might facilitate a text-based discussion of a topic of concern or interest to the group. The skills a coach could have are: setting norms for working together, active listening, understanding guidelines for dialogue, learning how to give and receive constructive feedback, using protocols for examining and improving student and teacher work, solving problems, setting goals, observing peers and building teams. Everyone in the CFG, participants and coaches, learn and expand their skills in this area.

The researcher was the coach in CFG meetings. She read about and studied the procedure and the protocols from different sources. She watched videos on the net and mailed to some coaches who were trained and were assigned as CFG coaches. Their experience and ideas were of great importance to the researcher. She undertook a role of a facilitator and an observer in the group. She kept her own journal and took notes during each meeting.

Data Analysis

As in any other qualitative study, the data collection and analysis occurred concurrently in this study. Baxter and Jack (2008) notes that the type of analysis engaged in will depend on the type of case study. Yin briefly describes five techniques for analysis: pattern matching, linking data to propositions, explanation building, time-series analysis, logic models, and cross-case synthesis. In contrast, Stake describes categorical aggregation and direct interpretation as types of analysis (Baxter and Jack, 2008, p.554). Data analysis, in this study, occurred through two phases. In the first phase, transcripts of CFG meetings were coded to identify a wide range of analytic themes and descriptive codes. In the second phase, teachers' journals were evaluated by discourse analysis. Direct interpretation was preferred. Table 10 shows the research questions and data sources triangulated.

Table 10 Research questions and data sources

Research Questions	Data Source 1	Data Source 2	Data Source 3
What are the attitudes and expectations of Turkish EFL teachers at Foreign Languages School of Mersin University concerning the effects of development-based INSET programme?	Questionnaire	Interviews	
In what areas do the teachers think they need training and development?	Questionnaire	Interviews	
In their own view, how has INSET programme followed by the Critical Friends Group (CFG) affected their professional development?	CFG Meetings	Journals	Teachers' Reflection
Has CFG has proved to be an efficient tool to evaluate the process teachers go through before and after the INSET?	CFG Meetings	Journals	Researcher's Notes
Is there any change in teachers' attitudes and expectations about language teaching and learning after the INSET programme?	CFG Meetings	Journals	Researcher's Notes

Data Analysis Procedures

The data analysis procedures for this study included coding, multiple sources, triangulation, and analytical procedures. A case-study approach using observations, interviews, and documents for collecting and analysing data is thought to be the most appropriate for research conducted in educational settings. A strong case can be made for using an approach that combines the collection of appropriate data with multiple sources of information and collaboration in most research regarding the effects of professional development on teacher performance. Data analysis followed a common format of written notes taken by the researcher during all observations. The researcher coded the notes taken during the study by identifying similarities and differences. Transcripts of the CFG sessions in which the teams used the protocols, the written feedback collected from the participants after most sessions, and field notes that document attendance, seating arrangements and non-verbal behaviour was the qualitative data that the study uses (Appendix I).

The researcher kept a field journal to record impressions from interviews, conversations and documents. The researcher discussed the progress and the CFG experience with the director as concerns, questions and problems occur. The researcher had participants review the transcripts from CFG meetings and interviews to check for accurate reporting.

A case study database was created. It included the data and a chain of evidence of the investigation. This database allowed an outside observer to understand the steps of the cases study. It included notes from interviews or document analysis, case study documents, researcher's notes and observations.

Chapter 3   Results and Discussion

The Attitudes and Expectations of Turkish EFL Teachers

The first research question was asked to find out the attitudes and expectations of Turkish EFL teachers at Foreign Languages School of Mersin University concerning the effects of development-based INSET programme. To this end, all instructors at the School of Foreign Languages were given a written questionnaire which consists of two parts. The first part of it questioned the background of the instructors; their age, gender, educational qualification, experience, and whether they had participated in any INSET programme. The second part was about the areas they feel they need development, the activities believed to be prior to the School and the effects of development-based INSET on their teaching would be. The instructors were also interviewed in order to find out their attitudes towards an INSET programme. Another online questionnaire was also conducted by the Teacher Training Unit of the School to investigate the areas they wanted to develop. The Tables 3 and 4 in Chapter 2 shows the demographic information and the needs analysis obtained from the online questionnaire.

The analysis of the written questionnaire revealed the fact that 24% of the instructors had participated in a development-based INSET programme Most of the in-service activities they joined were mandatory organized by the Ministry of Education. They were 2 to 3-day-long seminars given by a teacher trainer outside of school appointed by the Ministry. 86% of the instructors mentioned the need of an INSET programme designed for the School. Their expectations concerning the effects of the INSET are shown in Table 11.

Table 11 Expectations concerning the effects of the INSET

The INSET may	n:36
Increase my motivation	92%
Help me reflect on my teaching practices	74%
Upgrade my existing skills	68%
Provide opportunities to exchange experience and views	66%
Inform me about educational innovations	66%
Add additional qualifications	54%

Semi-structured interviews were also held by 20 instructors. They were asked what the benefit of an INSET programme for their own development would be and in what the areas they think they need training.

Increasing teachers' motivation was thought to be the leading effect of an INSET according to the questionnaire and semi-structured interviews. Similarly, increasing students' motivation was priority for most of the teachers. Therefore, they mentioned that they need to develop in terms of activities, new forms and methods of teaching which may be of help to them in their classrooms to improve the quality of teaching as well as the motivation.

Extract 4.1

I used to attend some seminars when I was teaching in my old school. It was compulsory to attend to those seminars for us. Therefore, I believe they were not effective. The trainers were unaware of the circumstances we were working and they were simply outsiders to our environment. For the INSET programme, I prefer a course designed according to our needs, which also enables us to reach to the students.

Extract 4.2

I will not need any more training if it is similar to those I have had so far. I need to develop myself; I need something new, which is unfortunately difficult in our field. I would like to use web-based materials to motivate my students. I want my students to think I am following the trends.

Extract 4.3

I have not had the chance to attend any INSET courses, or programmes. I started working in this institution right after I graduated from the university. I need to know if I am doing the right things. To share ideas with my colleagues, to learn alternative teaching techniques to adopt in my classroom would be great. I need feedback to be motivated.

Improving foreign language skills especially speaking and writing was believed to be another priority for the School. Teachers mentioned that they were curious about what their colleagues have been doing to improve the foreign language skills in other schools; how they manage to have their students communicate in English and improve their academic writing.

Extract 4.4

All through the year, we are struggling to teach our students English. We are giving them homework, worksheets, tests and so on. At the end, they still have difficulty to communicate, to talk in English. I wonder if this is a common problem in most of the institutions. I want to have an idea what they are doing to enable their students to speak in a foreign language. How is their curriculum designed? How many hours of writing lessons are they doing? Reflecting on what we are doing, how we are doing and whether we are doing the right thing is necessary.

According to the teachers, the programme would be more beneficial if it is an on-going organization, not only a few days activity. They stated that they would like to welcome instructors, professors from the university and out of the institution, who have been experts on specific areas. They also mentioned that practical information would be more beneficial for them than the theoretical instruction.

Extract 4.5

In two or three days or at one weekend, I do not think any training programme will be of success. It should be something in the long run, which needs to be supported by professionals outside of the School. Some kind of evaluation at the end of the course could be motivating.

Extract 4.6

> I want information that will be helpful to me in the classroom. I do not need
> any approach, theory etc. First, I would like to be listened about the problems I
> have encountered in the classrooms. My needs should be catered.

The instructors were also asked whether they believe in the benefit of INSET
programmes. Since some of them had had the opportunity to participate in training
organizations in their previous institutions, they had some positive remarks as well as
unfavourable reviews.

Extract 4.7

> Learning is a life-long process, especially when you are teaching a language.
> We need to develop at all times. Therefore, such organizations are helpful for
> teachers as long as they are well organized. I participated in some very good
> courses, which I believe I took advantage of, and in some very poorly designed
> short courses, which I was bore to death.

Extract 4.8

> Most of the courses I attended were compulsory. They were short-term. I do
> not think that they were beneficial. They were extra burden for me. I have been
> teaching 24 hours a week, I will not prefer to do extra activities unless they are
> professional.

Needs Analysis

The answers given to research questions 1 and 2 actually overlapped to some
extent. Teachers mainly felt the need of an INSET for themselves in the areas their
students need to improve. For example, they think that their students abstain to speak in
English, so they want to upgrade their skills to enable their students to communicate in
a foreign language. However, improving integrated language skills was the priority in
the questionnaires. They also wanted to be informed about recent educational
innovations so that they could eliminate this gap.

Extract 4.9

When our students start their departments after preparatory education, we are sometimes criticized by their professors that we could not get them to be able to speak or write English. After a year of instruction, it is true that most of our students lack productive skills, speaking and writing in English. We need to reconsider our curriculum. We need to be informed about possible new ways of improving the productive skills of the students.

Extract 4.10

Too much emphasis on grammar! This is what we have been doing wrong. Our students need to be able to understand texts of their fields. They need to understand what they listen to. Being able to speak English will be definitely more motivating for them. Well-planned syllabus for more communicative instruction should be experienced.

According to the online survey conducted by the In-service Teacher Training Unit, the teachers stated the following areas to be considered as the context of the INSET programme (Fig.4, in Chapter 2).

Improving integrated language skills, improving speaking skills, motivation in ELT, classroom management, use of technology for English classes, curriculum development, learner autonomy, improving listening skills, materials development, and language testing were mentioned.

In the interviews conducted, teachers stated that students need to improve foreign language skills, and focusing too much on grammar demotivates students and relatively the teachers after some time. Students expect to be able to speak English and know plenty of vocabulary to enable them to communicate both orally and in writing.

Teachers also mentioned that they have been teaching Generation Y, which means these students use technology at higher rates than people from other generations. Gen Xers and members of Generation Y were the first to grow up with computers in their homes. They use the Internet as their primary news source. Therefore, use of technology for English classrooms is a necessity not a luxury any more. Teachers thought that they need training on how to use the available technology for the sake of language learning.

Extract 4.10

I have heard about a program called 'moodle'. Some institutions apply such interactive online programs and I believe our students will benefit a lot from cyber instructions, homework or projects. We need some information about teaching with technology.

They believe that when students improve their foreign language skills, especially speaking, and when technology is integrated into language teaching, students will be motivated. However, they also mentioned that co-operation in education is necessary. The students will be taught in English in about 30% of their courses when they start their departments. If these students become aware of the fact that good proportion of English will help them in their studies, they pay more attention to their language courses. Therefore, some of the teachers think that co-operation with the departments can be of help to motivate the students. They suggested some seminars or short lectures in English for their students by their professors-to-be.

Extract 4.11

When students are informed why they learn English (not typical advantages of knowing a foreign language), I am sure they will have more motive. Cooperation between our school and the departments will be of great help for students. Seminars could be held by their professors. The students will hear why they should learn English, and how it will help them in their future career once again from someone they will be instructed in their departments.

Testing was another area teachers think that they need to develop. The quizzes are prepared by a group of instructors alternately during two academic years. Testing is an area which needs attention and professional help. Teachers said that they do not want students who only focus on examinations, and they want to utilize the educational aspect of testing.

INSET

The seminars organized under the INSET programme will be summarized below. All seminars were evaluated by the group, four of which were followed by the protocol related.

Classroom Evaluation

The seminar was given by a professor from Sociology Department. It was a sort of question-answer meeting. The presenter tried to sort out what problems teachers encounter most in the classrooms considering student profiles. He raised some issues such as students' background, students' native tongue, their tendency to learning a foreign language, their motivation levels, what goes well or what the most difficult part of being a teacher in this School is, and how to be an effective teacher.

The presenter was unfortunately not familiar with the field of language teaching or the atmosphere of the School; however, he looked at the issue from the perspective of a sociologist which was helpful. Classroom Evaluation and Success Analysis Protocol was adapted in the CFG meeting after this seminar (Appendix J).

Classroom Atmosphere and Cooperative Learning

The INSET event under this topic was, first, the video watching on Three Particularly Problematic Grammar Issues For English Language Learners, by Keith Folse, and secondly, the presentation by one of the professors of German Language Studies Department on 'The Priorities in Basic Language Skills in Foreign Language Teaching'. In both events, the classroom atmosphere was discussed and students' achievement was evaluated. How teachers could enable students to integrate into language learning and how peers can help each other in their studies were talked over. Classroom Atmosphere and Examining Student Work: A Constructivist Protocol (Appendix K) was used in the CFG meeting after these two INSET events were discussed. An observation schedule was made for Critical Friends so that they could observe each other's lesson and comment on the issues predetermined. Lesson observation checklists were used (Appendix M). However, the classroom atmosphere was the main topic to be kept in observers' mind.

Use of Technology in the Classroom

This seminar was actually planned to be the introduction of the "Moodle" application. How to use blogs, facebook, and twitter as a source of language instruction was also supposed to be discussed. However, the director of the school was rearranged the seminar as a workshop in which Microsoft Excel was introduced. The discussion was held informally after the workshop, and the instructors shared their experiences in group discussion. The use of technology in the classrooms was also the subject of one of the meetings of CFG. The researcher gave some examples of blogs, and how she uses the Facebook application as a source of material sharing, a field for cyber homework and project submission. The PhD dissertation by once the German instructors of the School about the use of "Moodle" on German teaching was discussed. It was planned to invite the colleague to one of the meetings.

Motivation

The seminar was given by the researcher on evaluating what the students of the School of Foreign Languages think of language learning and what teachers feel about their career. It was a study conducted by the researcher in the School, and it was presented in an international conference. First the study was presented, the results were discussed and suggestions were taken. Demotivation was one of the most important problems of the teachers. When they noticed what some students thought about language learning after evaluating the metaphors they had produced, they realized the difficulty of the situation, and the necessity of new and effective solutions to be taken. Some factors that cause students to become demotivated and frustrated during the stages of language learning were also talked over. Motivation and Dilemmas Protocol was followed the discussion in the CFG meeting (Appendix L).

Materials Development

This workshop started with the results of an MA Thesis on training and competence in materials development. It was a well organised session; the outcome of the study was interesting. The presenter, then, evaluated the materials needs of the institution, and the current work and effort the Materials Unit of the School had produced. The content of the course books was also discussed. Whether the students' background knowledge or cultural reservoir corresponds with the course books' was also focused.

CFG Meetings, Protocols and Participants

Six volunteer participants formed the CFG in this study. The group met regularly and seven protocols were used. After each INSET activity, the group evaluated the input and discussed about the benefits of the seminar or the workshop by the protocols and participants were asked to keep their journals under two predetermined headings, which were;

Interpretation: What was significant to you? Why?
 What inferences can you make about what we did or why we did it this way?

Application: How might I use this with my Critical Friends Group or in my classroom? What would I do differently?

The protocols served for the professional development of the teachers, and CFG was the tool to carry out the process, as well as the tool to evaluate the INSET programme. The four protocols used during the INSET programme were: Classroom Evaluation and Success Analysis Protocol, Classroom Atmosphere and Examining Student Work: A Constructivist Protocol, Observation Protocol and Constructivist Tuning Protocol, Motivation and Dilemmas Protocol. The meetings were audio-taped and the transcripts were evaluated. The transcripts of CFG meetings were also evaluated under these two headings.

After each INSET activity, the participants also wrote their reflections in their journals under the headings 'Interpretation' and 'Application' as well. The journals were given to the participants by the researcher with a pre-typed quote "Dear Diary,

What have I learned today? So what? How will I make use of what we have discussed in the meetings?"

CFG had also served as a tool to promote teachers' professional development. The participants were presented below. The names are pseudonyms.

ECE

Ece had been teaching English for about 11 years when she joined CFG. She had no prior INSET experience, and she was quick to volunteer for the opportunity to be a part of the group. She was a graduate of Language Teaching Department, but she hadn't had her post-graduate degree. She was the one who talked out loud about the need of teacher development activities in the School. She was working for the material development unit when the study was conducted.

SEMA

Sema was a graduate of 'Interpretation and Translation' department, so when she first started teaching at Mersin University, she said she had been like a fish out of water. She also mentioned that she needed some kind of orientation that might have given by the school and some in-service support while she was teaching. She was also quick to be a volunteer for the study. She had 5 year-experience by the time the study was conducted.

EDA

Eda was one of the experienced teachers with 12 years, and she had an MA on language teaching. Her previous experience was in Ministry of Education so she participated in some in-service training programmes given by the Ministry. She also worked in a private college, where she had the opportunity to join stuff development workshops.

CANAN

Canan had been teaching English for about 13 years at the time of the study. She had worked in the Ministry of Education for a short period. She is working for the material production unit of the School, and they are about to publish on a book which will be the course book of the Faculties soon. She had not had the chance to join any INSET courses.

SENA

Sena was an experienced teacher. She had a long history in high schools of Ministry of Education. She holds MA on Language Teaching. She participated in various conferences and seminars. She favours on-going learning. Her insights and experiences were of great contribution to the group. She presented in one of the seminars and talked about her study.

MERVE

Merve had been teaching 10 years by the time she participated in CFG. She had the chance to join a few short INSET programs before. She had worked for the testing unit of the School. She is now teaching in the Conservatory of the University.

Highlights of the Meetings and Protocols after the INSET

When the data from the CFG meetings, journals were coded, and after researcher's notes evaluated, four themes were detected. These were motivation, institutional constraints, integrating skills and classroom atmosphere, examining students' progress. These topics were determined after in-depth exploration of the each case. Four themes mostly mentioned were shown in Table 12. Relevant words, phrases, and comments for each theme were also noted.

Table 12 Main themes from the meetings and journals

Motivation	Institutional Constraints	Integrating Skills and Classroom Atmosphere	Examining Student Progress
•Demotivation, frustration, unwillingness •Lack of motivation •Students not taking active part in their learning •Need for motivational activities •Dense syllabus, only coursebook as a source •Lack of technological devices and programs	•Lack of support and understanding •Unfair work load •Lack of teacher autonomy •No one listening, needs not catered •Not taking part in the curriculum •Lack of encouragement •Lack of enthusiasm	• Less emphasis on grammar •Skills should be taught integrated •Interactive classrooms •More multi-media in teaching •Less teacher talking, more student participation •Target setting	•Portfolios, projects should be part of the instruction •Autonomous students •Students' Turkish skills are weak •No more tests •More productive activities, assignments •Progress repots are necessary

Motivation

Critical Friends were primarily concerned about the motivation problem of both the students and the teachers. When the contents of the meetings and the journals were analysed, motivation was the first and the most significant subject bothering the teachers. Participants agreed on the fact that when students are demotivated, it is inevitable for the teachers to be so. The seminar about motivation in the INSET programme was towards the detection of the problem. How students and teachers commented on learning and teaching English through metaphors was presented. The suggestions were made in the discussion session after the INSET. Remedies were discussed. The extracts below are from the journals written right after the meeting in which the seminar was evaluated.

Extract 4.12 (Ece)

Although I am teaching to a group of Tourism students, they are unaware of their needs and the importance of learning English for their future jobs. Most of them avoid speaking English during classes because they have a fear of failure. They believe that courses given in this school will not help them to be able to speak or communicate. They have had no background in language learning, which is pity.

Extract 4.13 (Merve)

When you follow a dense program, I mean syllabus, you have no time for extra activities, especially games, contests, and so on. The course book is the only source a teacher uses; no technology is available in the classrooms, not even a projector. So how come a student can enjoy the lessons. Even I become frustrated to do all the activities in the book. We have talked about some games and drama activities in the meeting and discussed the necessity of them in the seminar, but the curriculum must be revised in order to enable the extra-curricular activities.

Extract 4.14 (Eda)

I still have doubts if I can enable my students to be able to talk in English! It's a frustrating period, like swimming against the current. They are not studying enough and they seem not to be aware of the importance of English. After the discussion in the CFG meeting, we have come to a conclusion that students have to be given the responsibility of their own learning. We cannot teach them everything. Our goal has to be pushing them forward and motivating them. A classroom atmosphere where students can show what they learn and how they manage to do so is foremost important.

When the meeting transcripts and journals were evaluated, the comments on motivation were the leading ones. *Demotivation, lack of motivation, frustrating, unwilling, reluctant* were the phrases mostly encountered. One of the most important reasons for demotivation was said to be the stress to follow the syllabus for teachers and the impact of this on students, teaching for the exams, monotonous lessons, the quality of the students, no level determination exams, and teachers teaching the same classroom for the whole academic year. The biggest challenge for teachers was that most of them shared similar thoughts but they could not discuss the issue on a democratic, supportive environment except for the first time they did it in CFG meetings.

Extract 4.15 (Merve)

In these group meetings, we can discuss everything within the framework of student success, teaching tips, problems encountered, dilemmas lived. There is no criticism, no bossing, thoughts respected. This is motivating for teachers, unlike the atmosphere we have with the management. In these meetings, we may not learn great deal about teaching, or it is difficult for some of us to change their teaching styles; however, it is certain that we have been motivated, relieved and even enjoyed spending time with each other talking about the job we both try to do. At least, personally it helped me a lot!

Extract 4.16 (Canan)

New generation uses computers, texting within a split-second, comment on, like everything they read on the net, tweet simultaneously. They have no patience, lack responsibility, not easy to be focused. So we need to change the way we teach in order to get them into learning a language.

Extract 4.17 (Sema)

It is difficult to motivate students especially when we are very much concern about the program we have to follow. Students actually know the necessity of knowing a foreign language, but they get bored with all the rush in the class. After one of these meetings, I tried to have them play a game that I had learnt, and I noticed that they enjoyed a lot. We have to combine the courses with variety of activities, let the students get the joy of learning something new.

Extract 4.18 (Sena)

We used to have students who were enthusiastic and witty in the past. Now our students are as if they rue the day they were born. Most of them are not hardworking or quick of comprehension; they do not come to the university well equipped. So our job is getting harder. I teach something, and the other day they look at me as if they know nothing about it. Therefore, I think we need to adapt our methods, the approaches we use.

Institutional Constraints

As Richards and Farrell (2005) mention, language teaching institutions are expected to provide opportunities for their teachers to pursue professional development, and to provide conditions where teachers cooperate to achieve higher levels of learning among their students. To provide teachers with professional development opportunities has not been the priority of the School. The teachers are not allowed to participate in any conferences during the academic year; volunteers to attend MA or PhD programmes are not encouraged. This INSET occasion was the first opportunity in the history of the School, and the CFG process was planned according to the needs of instructors. The director of the school, however, redesigned the INSET programme. Six Critical Friends were totally contributed the study voluntarily. Despite everything, with this study, the school took the first step to provide an opportunity for its teachers.

During the meetings and in the journals, teachers constantly mentioned about the constraints they face with the management. They stated that they could not share any problems they encounter in the classrooms, or any negativity of the curriculum, testing, or the course book. The meetings had become a setting where the teachers talked about their frustrations, disappointments while working in the School. They have the desire for more understanding, helpful, encouraging administration. The transcripts of the meetings and the journals reveal this burnout.

Extract 4.19 (Merve)

During our meetings, I have realized that I am not the only one who encounters problems during classes at times, yet sharing them with friends helps. I wish I could do this with the administration because they are the one, who decides on the changes; who could help me with the problems which root in the syllabus, quizzes, course book and etc.

Extract 4.20 (Ece)

My dilemma is I like working in this School with my friends, however; I feel that my school administration does not like me. What have I done to him! We need peaceful, welcoming school where we can work as a team.

Extract 4.21 (Canan)

I long for a more supportive and peaceful environment to work. I know my responsibilities, I do my best for my students, and I do not want any reward for this. This is my job. I love it. I do not want to be scolded because of going to class with my cup of coffee, or going 2 minutes late.

Extract 4.22 (Sema)

Neat and clean corridors, classes; silent, punctual students; syllabus-oriented, course book and exam-focused lessons; rushing, complaining teachers are what we got in this School. We do not evaluate student and teacher learning, motivation and happiness.

Extract 4.23 (Eda)

We can do different things in the class hours, such as playing games, competitions, drama activities, project work. However, we have to follow the syllabus which is very dense. When we share our wishes about more relaxed class hours, no one seems to understand this need. We do not have any extra-curricular activities in this program. Then, we try to find out why our students get bored and why they are unwilling towards lessons.

Extract 4.24 (Sena)

> A school play, an English theatre, or a show can be a good idea for students to perform at the end of the academic year. Or, students can publish a 'School Gazette' in English. We should support them to use what they have learnt during their language education. They are at the university, they should understand that. Of course, it is easy to say this in this meeting. I do not think the director would agree with me. I may even be mocked!

Integrating Skills and Classroom Atmosphere

Participants seemed to share similar feelings that they put too much emphasis on grammar. For the last two years, students were taken to a speaking exam, but they thought that it was not enough. Teachers agreed that the course-book followed is satisfying and encourage multi-skill instruction. However, they admitted that they like teaching grammar and students are more content when they are taught so.

After the INSET seminar on 'Three Particularly Problematic Grammar Issues for English Language Learners', critical friends discussed the issue in the CFG meeting. They also noted their comments in their journals. One of the highlights from these transcripts was that the students' failure in some grammar points is due to their lack of Turkish grammar because they usually compare the rules with their native tongue. Teachers, also, teach likewise. According to some critical friends, the reason why students have hard times with the present perfect tense, for example, is because it is hard for a Turkish student to have a resemblance to this tense in his native language. For this reason, it was mentioned in the meetings and in some journals that after teaching grammar, students should see and use that rule in reading passages, in their conversations and in their writings until it is thoroughly understood. Some drama activities were shared in the meeting, and teachers decided to apply some of them in their classrooms and talked over in the following meeting. The reflections of the seminar were also brought out after teachers implemented what they had learnt.

Extract 4.25 (Canan)

> We are too much concerned about teaching grammar, and why we cannot teach is an issue we constantly discuss. We need to concentrate on all skills, and keep

in mind that language is better taught as a whole. The seminar was good! Ms Kate pointed at some issues which were worth thinking. The classroom atmosphere has an effect on learning. Students should realize that it is their task to learn, teachers are only the mentors.

Extract 4.26 (Ece)

In the writing lesson this week, I asked students to write about 'how to make a cake (omelette, etc.)'. The instructions were jumbled up and in groups they were supposed to put them in the right order. In limited time, the groups competed with each other and the winning group members were awarded with a chocolate. As we talked in one of the meetings, little awards always work. You cannot imagine how intriguing a chocolate can be! It went well and I was really satisfied with this activity. I emphasized on the use of the imperatives, do and don'ts, and new vocabulary were put on the charts on the walls. Students then talked about what kind of food they like and what food they can cook. I believe integration of the skills made the lesson both effective and enjoyable. In the second part, they were asked to write a postcard to their friends but they were unwilling this time. In my opinion, they find writing difficult because they try to learn English not by heart but by memorizing. What is more, they are too lazy to write a paragraph even in Turkish.

Extract 4.27 (Sema)

We put too much emphasis on grammar and the lessons are mostly teacher-centred. Moreover, the mechanic activities both from the course book and activity sheets bore students to death. We have been talking what we could do to make lessons more effective and the suggestions in these meetings sort of excite me; games, drama activities, competitions, etc. However, we have to rush through the syllabus and there is unfortunately no time for these.

Extract 4.28 (Eda)

Students like watching films or TV series and I believe they are really good for them even to revise their grammar. The scene in which a child screams from the toilet, 'I've finished mom!' could be kept in mind more easily than the present perfect tense rules. We have to allocate more time for multimedia activities for enabling students to develop their listening, vocabulary and even speaking.

Examining Student Progress

The last INSET seminar to be evaluated by the CFG participants was the one given by a professor of German Teaching on student profiles of Mersin University. Actually, the seminar was planned to be on bilingualism; however, the discussions canalized the seminar to our students' profile and their background. In the School of Foreign Languages, there are some bilingual students with Turkish-Arabic and Turkish-Kurdish. How much impact their bilingualism has on their English language learning is an area to be studied. In the meeting after the seminar, critical friends declared that these bilingual students in their classrooms generally have difficult times in their language progress. While some of them have pronunciation problems, others have difficulty in understanding grammar instruction. One reason for this came out to be students' poor Turkish grammar. Indeed, this is true for most of the students.

Extract 4.29 (Merve)

We start teaching English by the help of Turkish. I mean we teach rules by comparing them with Turkish. Our students, these days, have very poor Turkish skills because they are trained as test students. So when I say, 'put –s to after verbs in third single pronouns' while teaching affirmative sentences in present tense, I have to explain what that means. They question why the sentence 'I wakes up late at the weekends' is wrong because for most of them 'I' is a singular pronoun and what makes the difference is confusing.

Extract 4.30 (Canan)

We want our students to write first short paragraphs, and then compositions while they cannot write a proper piece of essay in Turkish. It was significant that in the seminar, there was a consensus about the importance of native tongue. If a student likes reading and writing in Turkish, he can do it in any foreign language he studies. We cannot change the education system in Turkey, but we can do something for our students to become more aware of what and how to study.

In the CFG meetings, after the seminar, participants discussed about the students' profile within 5 years. The common reflection was that in the past, students were coming to the university academically and behaviourally better equipped. Time is changing, students are changing and the education system in Turkey is constantly changing. As a part of this system, language teachers also suffer. It was agreed on that the curriculum could be designed according to the students' potential and background knowledge. The seminar only raised the issue once again, problems discussed. From the outcome of the meeting, it was clear that the testing system needs to be reconsidered.

Extract 4.31 (Ece)

Most of us do not favour multiple-choice testing system, but we apply them in our examinations. Students should be evaluated individually. Portfolio application can be a solution. We can give projects, and the students submit and present their studies.

Extract 4.32 (Sena)

I do not think that we, as a school, cannot evaluate the progress of our students. We do not have level system. I mean students start in one level and after each exam, whether being successful or not, they get through to the other level. I am not sure whether my student in an intermediate class has really intermediate level English. We need to evaluate students' success thoroughly, in all skills, in different assessment techniques. Teachers sharing the same class can get together, as we have been doing in CFG, and try to keep a track of each student by discussing their performance in the exams and in the lessons. It is a difficult task, but it will definitely work.

Extract 4.33 (Sema)

Students deserve to see their progress in English which, to me, is crucial for their motivation. Exams should not be the only criteria. To measure students' progress, meetings like CFG are helpful.

Peer-Observations

Being observed has always been stressful. Teachers do not want to invite anyone into their castles where they are the queens or kings. Behind the walls of the classrooms, they feel comfortable and secure so any intervention, even goodwill, can be regarded as an intrusion. So when critical friends were asked to observe each other, they were uncommitted at first. Most of them had never been observed before by their colleagues. They got paired and scheduled their programs for the observation. Observation checklist was provided (Appendix M).

The observation protocol was used by the participants. Pre and post observation sessions were held by the pairs. In the CFG meeting, the overall observation process was evaluated. The reflections were also noted down in the journals. The critical friends' common thought about the observations was that it was difficult at first, but totally helpful experience at the end. Participants found the post observation feedback sessions constructive as well.

Extract 4.34 (Ece)

At first being observed was stressful for me, but then I got used to it and forgot about the observer. I started feeling that she was like one of my students rather than an observer. I think her comments (both negative and positive ones) will help me improve myself in my teaching process.

Extract 4.35 (Sema)

Yesterday my friend and I observed each other and it was a nice day for both of us. At first it was an exciting situation but after a few minutes I forgot observing and being observed. This application was really useful. I requested my friend to record my lesson because I had always wanted to watch myself while teaching. After the lesson I watched it and observed once more my pronunciation, my relationship with the students. I noticed that I often use the expressions 'Ok!', 'Alright!' My friends' comments were also constructive. We both think that we made a true decision by joining the CFG.

Critical friends also stated that during observations, the atmosphere in the classrooms were not natural. Students were either quiet or too much talkative as they wanted to support their teachers in their observations. Teachers also mentioned that they tried to apply different things in the observed lesson so as to break the routine.

Extract 4.36 (Sena)

When my friend came to observe me, I did not feel anything strange. I took lots of tools with me to the class. Maybe this was unusual. I use tools and materials in the lessons but not in the same lesson one after another. I was not nervous. However, I guess I was trying to impress the observer.

Extract 4.37 (Eda)

When my friend was observing the lesson, students became so silent and stressful that I also felt tense. Normally the lessons are more enjoyable, but this one was not. Students thought I was observed by an inspector or so, and they kept quiet. In the lesson I observed, the students were vice versa. They thought the more they contributed the lesson the better their teacher would be graded. Whether stressful or not, I liked the idea of peer observation. We need another eye in our classrooms for the betterment of our teaching.

In the CFG meeting, the process was evaluated after pairs completed their observation. The idea of observing colleagues within the framework of predetermined items was favoured by the critical friends. The observer had little responsibility to the observed, and she was by no means judging, criticizing or evaluating the lesson. The observed had decided what an observer would focus on during the observation and the feedback was given accordingly. Therefore, the whole process was for the betterment of the teaching. It was also stated that learners were also observed indirectly and the classroom atmosphere became apparent.

Effects of CFG on Teachers' Professional Development

Many professional development programmes currently offered focus on simply exposing teachers to the latest theories and initiatives without providing the conditions (e.g., opportunities to practice, available time, feedback, etc.) required for them, which is actually the very heart of professional development. When teachers are to follow an intense program in the school or, when they worry about to keep up with the syllabus, they cannot benefit from these programmes thoroughly. Some institutions are consequently moving towards initiatives that provide a more dialogic and meaning-making view of teaching and learning, whereby teachers take a more active role in their own development, collaborating with others in their profession to address various pedagogical problems (Clark, 2001, p.172). Teachers are more likely to seek assistance and advice from other teachers than from resources in developing and enhancing their classroom practice (Poehner, 2009).

CFG model is a form of professional development that offers the opportunity for a collegial development, where teachers help and support their teacher friends to develop. CFG involve group conversations where all members contribute to helping a teacher look an issue in new ways. In institutions where professional development programmes are not encouraged and time for INSET programmes are not allocated, CFG can be an option.

In this research, CFG was fundamentally considered as a tool to measure the effects of the INSET programme coordinated by the School of Foreign Languages. CFG was also served as a model to provide professional development for group members.

The INSET programme was organized by the director of the School of Foreign Languages. Once or sometimes twice a month, a scholar was invited to the school and usually on Wednesday afternoons, all the instructors attended the seminars. The needs analysis results were taken into account but not profoundly. CFG members had meetings after each seminar, and they also got together as planned by the researcher. In these meetings, group members and the researcher first discussed about the seminar under predetermined headings. Notes were taken, experiences were shared, and observations were scheduled if any application was required. The protocols were also applied. The protocols helped the group to structure the discourse, kept the group focused and on track. Otherwise the meetings would have turned into small talk meetings.

Similar to the findings by researchers (Dunne & Honts, 1998; Nave 1998, 2000; Nefstead, 2009) in this study, teachers were positive about the experience and attributed personal and professional growth to their involvement in the CFG. From the transcripts of the meeting, the journals kept and the researcher's notes, it can be inferred that participants found CFG process effective because it was an adaptable process where teachers decided what they wanted to focus on. Teachers discovered the importance of analysing student work for their own personal growth. The CFG work was on-going, not a one-shot experience which enabled teachers to concentrate more on what they were doing. They stated that CFG contributed to a change in their thinking and classroom practices; collaboration increased with support in a small group of trusted-colleagues within their own school. For example, one of the participants decided to open a blog page for her class while another decided to start each day with a warm-up activity. Internet pages were shared; some conference dates and venues were noted in case one of the group members would like to participate. One important point mentioned in one of the meeting was that CFG was like a therapy for teachers. Teachers were content to join these meetings where they shared the problems, searched for solutions, suggested and learned activities and tactics. Therefore, CFG created a culture of collaboration and collegiality within the participants and hopefully within the school in the future.

Another point frequently mentioned during the meetings was that CFG motivated the participants. It created an atmosphere where experiences were shared. Friends listened to each other attentively, and noticed that they had common problems about the students' achievement and the management. They discussed students' work and tried to come up with ideas to enhance the achievement. The suggestions were noted down in order to be shared with the director. Practical ideas were also written down to be applied in the classroom. Journals revealed the data that when teachers feel motivated; they believe that students will be as well. Some participants believed that they managed to break the routine in their classrooms.

"I have never thought of going to class with a toilet paper in my life! But I did it and it worked. Students found the activity fun and we all enjoyed during the lesson. After playing the dictation game, they now look for more games and drama activities. As long as the syllabus allows, I will add such varieties in my lesson" (From the researcher's note, 2011).

One negative aspect mentioned in the journals was that while CFG raised the issues teachers concerned about, the school directors or programme coordinators were expected to listen and cooperate with the teachers. Nave (1998) noted that CFGs did not thrive when a professional culture that supported teacher collaboration and collegiality was absent; therefore, this professional culture must be supported by the leaderships of the school. Teachers believed that not being taken into account leads to being demotivated. The institutions' main concern is the education of the students, not the professional development of its instructors. This has been emphasized often, and in an underrated manner. Participants thought that there should be respect in the institution and among colleagues. They believed that CFG has an impact of motivating participants by mutual respect and support. The indirect intent of the professional development effort was to change the culture of the school toward a collaborative learning environment.

To assist in the research and gathering of current and pertinent information to enhance student learning and instructional practice, the researcher provided participants with two articles from educational journals. Participants were also free to share articles they would like to discuss. It was a fruitful moment to see that during the meetings in-depth discussions of new strategies in teaching was prevalent.

Has CFG has proved to be an efficient tool to evaluate the process teachers go through before and after the INSET?

Critical friends were given three reflection questions before and after the study. Their answers to these questions set light to the last two research questions. These are:

1- What are your initial/final perceptions in terms of your definition of a CFG?
2- How do you think the use of CFG may change/have changed your perceptions of your school, classroom and colleagues?
3- What changes in your instructional strategies will/have occurred as a result of your participation in CFG?

The first reflection question aimed at eliciting the participants' perceptions regarding the definition of a CFG. The teachers were given a brief definition of CFG at the very beginning of the study. The process was explained and examples were given. The next question was about how they thought the use of Critical Friends Group might and would change their perceptions of their school, classroom and colleagues. The last question investigates the changes in teachers' instructional strategies as a result of participating in CFG, both as a process and a tool to evaluate the INSET programme.

All participants expected the CFG to be a group of friends, volunteers trying to discuss reflectively to make the teaching-learning process more effective. They mentioned that the group was a place where they shared ideas, brainstormed on various topics as they anticipated. CFG was also defined as a kind of group in which there are professional, enthusiastic teachers working cooperatively and sharing ideas democratically in a friendly atmosphere. The members try to develop different ways to improve teaching-learning process, which also contributes to teacher development. Their final belief about the CFG was positive. They believed it was motivating, and encouraging getting together with a group of friends and moving on more professionally afterwards. One critic was about the number of meetings being insufficient. More meetings were desired.

Extract 4.38 (Sema)

As I expected at the beginning, it was a nice experience for me as a language teacher. I learned some new activities to be applied in the class. I always believe sharing ideas and knowledge are a must among teachers because as we go on teaching, we go on learning and we should be generous about sharing our useful ideas. CFG was a good example and I think we can create our own CFG - it's necessary to be volunteers- in other years and make regular studies. Experienced or less experienced, all we have different approaches in classes and working on these make us more conscious teachers, I think.

Extract 4.39 (Canan)

CFG provided a process of self-observation and self-questioning for teachers. Teachers gather to share experiences, applicable methods, techniques and materials. Teachers generally confine themselves to a routine way of teaching in the classroom. However, they find it difficult to question the ongoing techniques or materials, even when they hinder the teaching process. Teachers usually tend to follow conventional methods until change is inevitable. CFG lead the teacher to recognize the problem and share it with colleagues. Thus, the group was able to discuss it and came up with different ideas. These ideas would probably help to solve the problem and make the teaching process better and more efficient.

The teachers believed that CFG process helped them professionally. It was meant to be the tool to evaluate the INSET programme; however, the process itself was satisfactory. The INSET programme was evaluated and teachers tried to get most out of it by discussions and comments. Therefore, both the INSET and the CFG process were effective, and changed the teachers' attitudes towards professional development activities.

Extract 4.40 (Canan)

I think CFG made a significant contribution to our professional development. As teachers, we reflected on the problems and solutions. Collaborative work added value to the teaching process. Discussing a problem or receiving feedback after an observation was supportive. During our meetings, I have realized that I am not the only one who encounters problems during classes at times, yet sharing them with friends helps. As a result of my participation in CFG, sharing knowledge and opinions about teaching with my colleagues appeals to me now.

Extract 4.41 (Sema)

CFG made me be more active again. Students or the working conditions, terrible management, etc. had stolen all my light for the last few years. This year, thanks to God I had a nice main course class and I could do what I wanted- as much as possible (Always in a mood that I would be warned by the management because of noise we made during the activities) I applied what I learned in CFG and it really worked. My students were happy with it. But I must confess it was enjoyable thanks to my students. I think I can't apply all these activities with students thinking games are for children and it's stupid.

Extract 4.42 (Ece)

Thanks to CFG, some of my perceptions of my teaching environment have changed. I've learned that every colleague has something to share with the other, which helps them see their individual needs and improve different teaching techniques. To be honest, I've always tried to be a sensitive and responsible teacher but as a result of my participation in CFG, I've started to think more critically about teaching. Especially in that period I was more creative and productive in my work because I've made use of my colleagues' experiences and practices.

Extract 4.43 (Merve)

Frankly, I cannot say that there is any change in my language teaching approaches and techniques. I know what to do to motivate the students and make learning process more enjoyable, and I am trying to do so. However, this whole process made me realize how much support and common-sense we need as teachers in this institution. It does not matter how competent a teacher has been, she needs motivation and a slow pace curriculum.

Extract 4.44 (Sena)

It seems that our CFG is democratic. We appear to feel hunger for more professional growth. I hope that we will be able to work as a team in the future. When we came together, everyone gave attention to the person speaking, hoping to exchange ideas and opinions. I think our discussions were energetic and we probably felt that we had a very important responsibility. I will try to improve the situations in my class and at my school. The reflections in the meetings will help me become a better learner and a teacher.

Extract 4.45 (Eda)

I have been teaching English for about 11 years in different institutions. I have always felt the need to develop myself, learn new things, and become a better teacher. This group work has reminded me of not giving up participating in professional development activities. I felt energized.

The responses to reflective questions before and after the study and critical friends' journals indicated that CFG was regarded as an effective tool both to evaluate the INSET activities and to create a professional learning community to support and foster teaching and learning. Participants of the study often mentioned the terms constructive, effective, reflective, democratic, comfortable environment for the CFG process. They found it useful for their professional development.

Is there any change in teachers' attitudes and expectations about language teaching and learning after the INSET programme?

The INSET programme organized by the school was found to be insufficient in general by the participant teachers. Problems, concerns, and current situation of the students and the school were discussed in the seminars; however, possible ways, suggestions or remedies were hardly introduced. Critical Friends indicated that when the INSET programme was evaluated in CFG meetings, it was said to be more efficient and more was taken out of the seminars. They would like to join other professional teacher development programmes in the future if possible. CFG was mainly considered as a form of INSET, rather than a tool for evaluation by the participant teachers. When the data was considered, INSET followed by a CFG was highly favoured. The attitudes of the participants were positive. The teachers in this research study voluntarily participated after they were asked whether they would be interested in contributing to a research study of this nature. Voluntary participation to the study may have had an impact on this overall positive attitude, as in the studies of Güçeri (2005) and Şeker (2007).

Extract 4.46 (Canan)

I really liked the professional atmosphere in our school. During the seminars, I had the chance to reconsider the issues discussed, and it was another chance to get together with my friends afterwards to exchange ideas. I used to find in-service programmes boring and unnecessary. However, I believe I benefited from this study. I will attend

Exract 4.47 (Eda)

I think CFG changed my perceptions of my classroom and colleagues. When I talked with them, I realized that I am not the only one who faces challenges in the classroom. All of us sometimes have difficulties in achieving our goals. I have come up with ideas that will help me solve the problems while exchanging ideas. Thus I can develop effective instructional strategies.

Extract 4.48 (Sena)

One of our colleagues shared VAK Learning Styles Self-Assessment Questionnaire with the group. I have known Multiple Intelligences Theory for a long time, but I have never applied the theory in my classes efficiently. Giving the questionnaire will help students realize their own learning styles and develop learning strategies. Thanks to the group spirit that I have revived what I have been postponing for so long.

Extract 4.49 (Merve)

That's the best part of teaching- the learning. I think this quote is so very much suitable for this study. Learning never stops, that's what I have expected from my job. I realized that I have become a little bit rusty in my teaching. This INSET was useful, but not enough. CFG was a good initiative. I could have benefited more if I was not so burned out in the school thanks to the director.

When non-participant teachers' views and Critical Friends' are taken into account, the impact of the CFG is clearly seen. Non-participant teachers' expectations were not met. The questionnaire they filled after each seminar, the interviews held by the researcher revealed their thoughts.

Non-participant Teachers' View after the INSET

The INSET seminars were thoroughly discussed by participant teachers in CFG meetings; related protocols were used to guide the discussions, and the CFG members tried to get most out of the programme by collaborating and supporting each other. They observed their partners' lessons and gave constructive feedback afterwards. The word 'critical friend' meant a colleague who supported, shared, listened, suggested, collaborated, and helped. The extracts reveal the positive impact of this implication on participants. Non-participant teachers only attended the seminars and filled in the questionnaire after each one. They had no chance to discuss what had been talked. The researcher interviewed ten of the instructors within a week after each seminar. The overall impression was given under 3 headings. These were lack of follow-up after the INSET, dominance of theoretical knowledge, not practical ideas, and lack of collaboration.

Follow-up after the INSET

After an INSET course ends, the evaluation of the programme against its objectives is often neglected. "Follow-up-evaluation" or "tracer" studies exploring outcomes and long-term effects of particular INSET activities are rare both in the Turkish context and in the language education field (Mathew 2006, cited in Uysal, 2012). The INSET programme in this study was not an exception according to participants who did not join CFG.

Extract 4.50

I have been waiting for this INSET programme, wondering how it will address my needs. The speakers are specialized in their fields, and what they tried to convey was important. However, after the INSET, I went back to my normal routine teaching in my classroom as usual.

Extract 4.51

The discussion sessions after the seminars were not enough. I felt as if I have more to say, to share and to show. Most of my colleagues just listened to the speakers silently but I wondered what their opinions were.

Extract 4.52

The intention was remarkable. As a school, this had been the first time we came together for our professional development. But how can I develop if I just listened to someone for an hour and then went back to my classroom without digesting what was recommended. I felt the need for post seminar activities.

Extract 4.53

I do not want to be too pessimistic, but I do not think this programme would be useful for our teaching practices or constructive for our institutional concerns. Most seminars were given by outsiders who are unaware of the realities this institution and the field of English language teaching has. The director should have considered what we thought after the seminars, if they were effective, met our needs, applicable and so on. Otherwise they were similar with the ones I attended during my teaching years at Ministry of Education schools.

Practice versus Theory

Studies show that Turkish INSET programs follow a pure transmission model to teach theoretical knowledge without allowing teachers to take active participation in their learning, reflect on their experiences, or implement what they learn (Bayrakçı 2009; Odabaşı, Çimer et al., 2010; Uysal, 2012). Similar comments were made by the teachers after the INSET programme.

Extract 4.54

Most teacher development activities, as far as I have experienced, are given by trainers or someone in higher status. Most of the time theory dominates the content. I need practical advice; suggestions that will make me progress in my teaching and, therefore, help my students succeed. First two seminars were not what I looked forward to.

Extract 4.55

In the INSET circle, evaluation is an important part. However, we did not have any chance to do it after the seminars. I have been teaching English for years. What I need is some refreshment in my teaching practices, not theoretical knowledge.

Extract 4.56

I need upgrading my existing skills. I am an experienced teacher at a certain age, so, learning new skills or improving my knowledge is not possible with teacher training programmes. I need back up and an opportunity to exchange experience and views. No more teaching theory please. We need reflection.

Extract 4.57

No matter how much theory is given, a teacher acts according to classroom situations she encounters. Some of the seminars given so far have not reflected what I am experiencing in the classroom. The speakers determined the state of some teaching and learning procedures. I enjoyed listening to them. There were right evaluations but practicing them may differ. I would prefer more discussions with the presenter and my colleagues after the seminars.

Extract 4.58

Most training programmes I have attended so far have been one way. There is always a presenter or trainer who tries to talk about what we can do, or we should do to make learner learn. This is not that simple. Theory is one aspect of teaching, and practice is the other. We need more support in practice. This can be done by in many ways. Workshops, group discussions and observations are what I can suggest. Thus, I believe this programme could have been supported by such applications in order to observe the outcome. We need reflection.

Lack of Collaboration

An INSET should enable teachers to socially-construct new information building upon their prior knowledge through reflections on current beliefs, collaborations, and social interactions (Reagan & Osborn, cited in Uysal, 2012). Contrary to CFG model, the traditional INSET model which was implemented in this study lacked collaboration and reflection among colleagues.

Extract 4.59

I have not attended many seminars; however, my impression is that once you get into the classroom, you forget all about it, and you feel safe to follow the way you often do. Collaboration, after or during the seminars, may have some effect on my teaching. By observing more experienced friends I can have clues on the situations we have encountered. I always felt the need of guidance when I first started teaching in this institution. I tried to find my own way to deal with problems. Now I have fewer obstacles, but I am not sure if I am on the right track. The seminars given under the INSET programme is a start.

Extract 4.60

My partner has been attending group discussions since the seminars started. They have been coming together and evaluating what was discussed. She started doing more motivating activities in the classroom and students are talking about them enthusiastically. She told me that during the meetings they share opinions with other participants, reflect over the sessions, keep journals, and try to be supportive. I just listen to the presenter in each seminar and go back to my routine. I liked the idea of collaboration. I am a candidate for the next CFG.

Extract 4.61

I am aware of the need of professional development in my career. Improving my grammar, vocabulary, phonology, writing skills and etc. is not practical and rational to me. I want to share ideas and collaborate with my colleagues, reflect on my performance in order to further develop as professional. This INSET programme is similar to most programmes we were forced to join in Ministry of Education schools.

Researcher's Notes

During the CFG meetings, the researcher acted as the member of the group and the moderator. Since the CFG design encourages teacher-driven discussion, the researcher's role was to present the meeting content and to enable each participant to take equal turns. She joined the discussions when sharing experiences or suggestions. She was the facilitator and the observer. She took notes in each meeting, wrote down the gist of the meetings, prominent issues, comments about the INSET, CFG, the classrooms and the students.

The researcher used a form for each meeting to take notes. Agenda items and the purpose of the meetings were written down (Appendix N). Since the meetings were audiotaped and the transcripts were evaluated afterwards, the researcher mainly focused on the issues which were constantly raised and remarkable for the implementation of CFG.

Institutional impediments made its mark on most of the meetings. Teachers constantly indicated the need of support from the institution. They mentioned that the management should consider arranging meetings like CFGs and consult teachers' opinions about the curriculum, textbooks, syllabus, and exams. Teachers' motivation needs to be taken into consideration. General perception of the teachers about the institution was that they are not valued. They are looking for a more understanding, supportive and peaceful atmosphere, which will foster both student and teacher learning indirectly. The atmosphere the CFG created enabled teachers to reveal their thoughts and concerns freely, which was the outstanding feature of this study. The friends supported each other, listened to attentively, and provided constructive feedback whenever necessary. As mentioned in the literature, when teachers are provided professional support and guidance, they raise awareness on their professional applications, build confidence and as a result they are empowered and they may change (Christison & Stoller, 1997; Kelly, 2007; Curry, 2008). However, these cannot be achieved without the administrative support.

Intense syllabus and keeping up with the program was another key issue teachers brought up in the meetings. They stated that they felt exhausted to follow the syllabus so as the students. Rushing in the classroom to teach as much as possible as dedicated teachers, and expecting the students to show similar effort and enthusiasm, but being disappointed at the end were the critical issues discussed in the meetings. The lack of time was also a problem to pursue any professional development activities. Once again, the administration should allocate time for extra-curricular activities for teachers. In this way, the necessary follow-up and reflection would be supplied for any in-service course. In this sense, CFG is a practical and effective model for evaluating the outcomes of INSET courses.

As for the CFG procedure, the comments were mainly focused on the idea of working in a group where there is no hierarchy and each member respecting one another. Learning from each other more or less was often mentioned, but sharing professional concerns and sometimes even personal issues were highly valued and appreciated. They mentioned that they discussed their feelings as well as their thoughts, which was like a therapy most of the time. It was clear that teachers tried to understand one another's viewpoints, most members were open to new ideas or ways of thinking, the group looked at issues from multiple perspectives and they indicated that they wanted to share what they learnt from this team with others outside the team. They said that the act of working collaboratively resulted in greater learning for each of them than if they had worked alone.

The CFG actually acted as a role of a professional learning community where teachers were voluntarily involved rather than a tool to evaluate the INSET programme. One reason for this might be the programme having been implemented not according to needs analysis but according to the management decisions. The programme could not reflect totally the teachers' needs in the institution but general concerns in language teaching. Therefore, the discussions were superficial and the reflections of the INSET in the classrooms were merely observed. CFG meetings served as feedback sessions of the seminars, which were beneficial as long as the presenters and the management staff of the institution involved in. When the other participants were considered, CFG teachers benefited more from the INSET programme as they had the chance to evaluate the seminars in the meetings with the protocols provided.

Each participant's views will be highlighted briefly from the researcher's point of view:

ECE: Striving for a respect for her professional identity

In the case of Ece, the growth was obvious. She contributed a lot to the meetings. She was always the first teacher who tried suggested activities or read recommended articles.

"I think being a member of this CFG encouraged me to be more creative while teaching. It also showed me that I can learn from my students. Sharing experiences with my colleagues was priceless. Growth never stops in learning." (Ece, from journal entry 2011)

Her dilemma was about students' performance. She believed that as teachers, they try to do their best for students. However, she was not about the outcome. She was concerned with gaining a deeper understanding of student learning. She liked the meeting when students' works were examined. She was also concerned with how she could enhance her practice by addressing students' multiple learning styles, different backgrounds, and interests. She said,

"My experiences and the outcomes from these meetings have led me believe in more student-centred learning. The curriculum we follow is teacher-centred and test-oriented. We should give more responsibility to our students." (Ece, from CFG meeting 2011)

She noted in her journal that applying variety of activities with her students after CFG meetings changed the atmosphere of her classroom. To her, students noticed that they could use the language they learned, so they began to take the control of their own learning.

Ece's notes revealed the fact that the CFG provided her with the opportunity to look at her teaching in a different way. She was more likely to take risks in her classroom. She believed, in this way, she gained more students than before. Ece's enthusiasm for professional development programmes, including CFG, can be explained as a desire to establish a professional identity. She noted that her expertise as a teacher did not seem to be fully appreciated by the school management. She was, therefore, volunteer for this group and she believed her enthusiasm, expertise, experiences were valued by the group members, something which she never felt in the school before.

"I am a graduate of a prestigious university, and I have been teaching English for years. Not having a title before my name or not being a faculty member does not mean that I am not good in my career. I am a professional by all means. I want to work in a professional environment." (Ece, from journal entry, 2011)

SEMA: Making her own way in teaching

"The group helped me to feel that I am more or less on the right track. I really appreciated the group members listening to my views and offering suggestions. I was the least experienced teacher in the group, but I think the most benefited of all." (Sema, from journal entry 2011)

The School of Foreign Languages is the first institution Sema started working. She said she had no induction, or any information about the system of the school. She was like a fish out of water at the first months of her teaching. She was a graduate of 'Translation and Interpretation' department, so she always felt incompleteness in the way she teaches. She noted that she felt so limited with the way she handled her class. She was quick to volunteer for the study, and eager to take down notes in her journal, and participated as much as possible in the discussions.

According to her, 5-year teaching experience is not enough and she believes she needs to deepen her content knowledge, promote quality teaching, keep up to date with new teaching methods and motivate students. CFG has been a start for her. She thinks her participation in this group enhanced her skills, and she said she learnt so much in the process.

Her dilemma was the lack of feedback she receives. She noted that she has tried some ways of teaching, and good or bad, she has stuck on one or two ways that she thinks that work. She feels the need to join more professional activities, workshops, seminars, certificate programmes, and so on.

"When I tried the "Running Dictation" activity in my class, I noticed that variety is needed in my teaching. Students were really motivated; even I had so much fun. No need to worry to lose control of the classroom, then." (Sema, from journal entry 2011)

"It is very nice to be with my colleagues in these meetings and being listened to! I am looking forward to be observed as well. It will be the first time that another teacher will observe me and my class. A little bit unsettling, but good!" (Sema, from researcher's note, 2011)

EDA: Waiting for the support to start her PhD

Eda was one of the experienced teachers of the group. She started working in the Language School of a university after graduation and before this school she had worked in a private college. She had the chance to join some training programmes. She holds an MA in ELT. She was upset about not being able to continue her studies. She emphasized frequently the importance of the support of the institutions for professional development of their teachers.

"We should have more input into our own professional development. However, without the support of the school directors, it seems impossible. With this work load and rigid lesson schedule, it is difficult to develop a plan for my professional learning. The INSET organized in the school was a start but I do not believe it is sufficient. I have

really enjoyed participating in CFG even it brought some extra work. The INSET meant something with CFG process." (Eda, from journal entry, 2011)

Eda's dilemma was not being professionalized in one group of students. Her programme has been changing almost every year. Since she started teaching in the school, she has taught to preparatory students, vocational school students, faculty school students using different course books and assessing in different ways. She wants to teach to the same group of students at least for two years to specialize.

She liked the idea of using protocols in the meetings because she thinks, otherwise, group work turns into small talk sessions.

"*I know that without some sort of guidelines, such as protocols, the group discussions take so long and mostly drift away from the main point. Teachers start complaining about the students, dense syllabus to follow and etc. When we used protocols in this study, we listened to each other more, evaluated students' performance better and suggested rational ideas*". (Eda, from journal entry 2011)

"*Attending conference sessions, reading journals always provides insights into my teaching. This study reminded me to invest into my professional development.*" (Eda, from CFG meetings 2011)

CANAN: Believing in the benefit of collegiality

Canan believed that CFG was worth their efforts and was a means for professional development. She thinks an important benefit of CFG was to promote collegiality among teachers in the school.

"*I think CFG enabled us to learn a great deal about each other and to develop a closer professional and personal relationship. Learning new teaching methods and applying them in our teaching style is not that easy. I think it takes time and will to do it. However, CFG promoted sharing and supporting environment that we long for.*" (Canan, from journal entry 2011)

Canan indicated both in the meetings and in her journal that CFG process enabled her to take risks in her teaching, which she had not done for so long. She complained about the monotony in the way she teaches. However, being part of this study helped her to try something different.

"Each time I meet with colleagues in the CFG, I get so inspired and motivated to try new things or approach something in a different way." (Canan, from CFG meeting 2010)

Canan was chosen in a group that was responsible to write a book to be used for Vocational Schools and Faculties. Her dilemma was that she had no prior experience in writing a course book. She is an experienced teacher, but she is not an author. To her, preparing a course book is an important task which should be realized by experts. She shared her concerns in the meetings. She also used the meetings as a place to see how the land lies. She said she took what teachers suggested for the students into consideration.

Canan favours any form of training and development programmes. Therefore, she was happy to join the group and hopeful for the future organizations that the school might hold. Her expectation was that for the future INSET organizations, scholars who are experts or experienced in English language teaching would be invited from different universities or institutions. Moreover, she hopes for the next time needs analysis would be taken into account more seriously.

"In one of the CFG meetings, we talked about "moodle", which is the programme I have not heard before. It took my attention a lot. We agreed on that we have to keep up with the technology. It would have been great if this INSET had included a session on the use of the technology in language teaching." (Canan, from researcher's notes 2011)

SENA: Sharing expertise

Sena was the most experienced member of CFG. She has an insatiable desire for knowledge. She joins the conferences, present her studies that she conducts in her classrooms, reads recent articles. She holds a MA, and looking for the chance to do her PhD. She shared her insights with other members with a sense of mission.

Sena looked at CFG as an opportunity to share her expertise and to elicit interesting ideas from colleagues but she was also interested in developing her own level of expertise with CFG because she found that the protocols themselves gave her ideas for how she could structure interactions in her classroom. Sena's dilemma was concerned the performance of her students. She believed she taught every possible thing in the syllabus. However, the students were not as successful as she wanted them to be. This was the concern of almost all members, but Sena mentioned this issue regularly in the meetings. She believes that nowadays students do not know how to study, they are ignorant and indifferent. She mentioned two-way interaction in the classroom.

"*We used to have students who were enthusiastic to learn English. Today, most students are indifferent and they are test-focused. Language cannot be learned by doing tests. You need to practice a lot. Only the teacher's effort is not enough.*" (Sena, from CFG meetings 2011)

She noted in her journal that the best professional development challenges teachers' assumptions about learning and engages them in extending skills. Most INSET programmes she had joined were mandatory and short-termed. She believes she got something from each of them, but she prefers more challenging and innovative programmes. Sena liked the idea of professional learning communities, and believes in the practical aspect of such gatherings. She also mentioned the importance and the effectiveness of focusing on student work rather than abstract discussions of teaching.

"*Professional teacher development can occur when teachers are actively involved in their development; and when they concentrate on instructional practices.*" (Sena, from journal entry 2011)

MERVE: Trying to get rid of the burn-out

Merve was the member of CFG who was concerned about the institutional constraints the most. She does not believe that any INSET can be successful without administrative support. She thought that the school environment lacks support and common-sense. She was unhappy and burn-out during the time the study was conducted.

For Merve, there was too much pressure on the instructors. The distribution of the workload was not fair. She is a kind of teacher who never regards teaching burdensome. However, her duty in the testing unit and the conflicts she experienced with the head of the unit was tiring for her. Therefore, her participation in the study was meant a lot.

The CFG meetings turned out to be a reminder of various practices that Merve had learned during her previous trainings. She shared her ideas and experience with the colleagues. She was happy to be listened to. Her dilemma was that students are listened to attentively by their teachers, but no one listens to teachers' concerns and problems in the school.

"*I did not think I could get any benefit from this study. Fortunately, my friends were very supportive and caring. I noticed the inevitable relief of exchanging ideas during the meetings. I have learned what my friends experience with their students, and how they try to overcome the problems they encounter. This group was like a therapy.*" (Merve, from CFG meetings 2011)

For the professional development of teachers, she emphasized that teachers should decide on the time, area, method they want. Nothing should be mandatory. After 5 to10 years of teaching, she believes it is difficult to create a change in teachers' practices unless they are willing and enthusiastic.

"*Many teachers find that after a year or two in the classroom, each day is very much like the next, and there are few opportunities for doing new and interesting things. This routine should not be allowed by the institutions; otherwise it becomes harder to enable teachers to develop professionally. Teachers should be offered opportunities and support to pick up suitable ways to develop and keep fresh in the way they teach and of course lean.*" (Merve, from journal entry 2011)

Summary

In this chapter, the researcher presented the findings from the analysis and interpretation of the data from the questionnaire, interviews, participants' journals, CFG meetings and her notes. This information was used to answer the research questions of the study.

The questionnaires, written and on-line, and the interviews helped the researcher to give response to the first two questions, which were 'In what areas do the teachers think they need training and development?' and 'In their own view, how has INSET programme followed by the Critical Friends Group (CFG) affected their professional development? The importance of needs analysis in any INSET programme or course once again emerged from this study. The teachers whose needs are analysed expect them to be catered and taken into account. The expectations should be met. Otherwise, positive attitudes towards professional development activities could not be maintained.

The participant journals, meeting transcripts, and the researcher's notes were evaluated to find out whether INSET programme followed by the CFG affected the participants' professional development, if CFG was proved to be an efficient tool to evaluate the process teachers went through before and after the INSET, and whether there was any change in teachers' attitudes and expectations about language teaching and learning after the INSET programme.

The involvement and the contentment of the participant teachers in CFG were remarkable. The group developed a professional learning community through the implementation of CFG. It was a democratic and supportive atmosphere to evaluate the INSET programme as well as a process which triggered professional development. Adequate feedback after each INSET seminar was supplied. CFG was proved to be an efficient tool for various reasons. First, it satisfied the participants' growing need for feedback from colleagues. Second, the participants enjoyed their CFG experience because it helped them to learn from their partners. The CFG experience provided good opportunities for exchanging professional ideas in a comfortable atmosphere as in the study of Vo & Nguyen (2008). Finally, the six participants revealed that they felt positive about the process because they believed that the CFG process had helped to build up good work and social relationships, resulting in a 'sense of community' and a mutual understanding. Within this study, the many benefits of CFG reported in previous studies have been confirmed in a Turkish context.

As for the change of the expectations and the attitudes, the data reported positive results. However, the change in attitudes towards the INSET course was difficult to determine since the INSET did not satisfy the expectations. It was the first INSET programme organized in the institution; it was like a chain of seminars. The teachers in the school were delighted with the idea of a course for their professional development. Their expectations about language teaching might have been high. It is not realistic for INSET courses to set goals for a change in language teaching. An INSET can provide teachers with alternative and innovative ways of teaching, but it takes time and desire for a teacher to change. Nevertheless, teachers in the study mentioned that they believe any activity conducted for the teachers' development would be beneficial. CFG participants, on the other hand, would like to join more groups, seminars, workshops provided that those activities could facilitate their development. As mentioned before, teachers are learners of language teaching. It is a life-long and on-going process, and every teacher is responsible for her own development.

Chapter 4   Conclusion

Summary of the Study and Evaluation of Research Questions

The purpose of the study was to evaluate the impact of INSET programme on professional development of EFL teachers through the CFG. This study also focused on the formation and implementation of CFGs at Mersin University, the School of Foreign Languages, and it was aimed to understand the process of developing a professional learning community through the CFG.

The study aimed to find answers to the following questions:

1-   What are the attitudes and expectations of Turkish EFL teachers at Foreign Languages School of Mersin University concerning the effects of development-based INSET programme?

2-   In what areas do the teachers think they need training and development?

3-   In their own view, how has INSET programme followed by the Critical Friends Group (CFG) affected their professional development?

4-   Has CFG has proved to be an efficient tool to evaluate the process teachers go through before and after the INSET?

5-   Is there any change in teachers' attitudes and expectations about language teaching and learning after the INSET programme?

The researcher aimed at stimulating the professional development of teachers in the institution. To this end, a development-based INSET program was organized for the instructors who wanted to explore their own professional development, as well as to facilitate mentor development. The attitudes and expectations of the teachers towards an INSET programme were inquired by a questionnaire at the beginning of the study, and the content of the INSET programme was determined accordingly. The subjects that the teachers thought to have priority in the INSET programme were revealed in Figure 3 in Chapter 1. Interviews were also held in the school to uncover the opinions and ideas of the teachers about in-service teacher training courses and what they expect from the one which was to be planned for themselves. The data gathered from the questionnaires, both written and online, and the extracts of the interviews give answers to the first two research questions of the study. The Table 11 in Chapter 2 shows the expectations of the teachers concerning the effects of the INSET.

The overall impression of the teachers towards INSET programmes was positive. The participants of the study were aware of the importance of teacher development and they considered this process as a life-long learning. Some of the teachers in the school had some experience of joining training programmes in their previous institutions; however, most of the instructors had not had any teacher development courses after their graduation from the university. They were aware of the need for on-going renewal of professional skills and knowledge and they stated that, at pre-service level, it is not possible to be provided everything they need to know. They indicated that teaching constantly changes and they have to upgrade their skills and knowledge. There was genuine interest expressed in their professional development among the instructors. The extracts in Chapter 2 reveal this interest.

The participants involved in the CFG study were six English instructors working at the school. The Critical Friends Group (CFG) was the tool to evaluate the impact of the programme and it also served as a tool to provide effective feedback and strong support for the teachers in their practices in the classrooms.

A case-study design was utilized. Participant teachers had eight CFG meetings in which they evaluated five seminars given as a part of the INSET programme and four protocols were used to guide the teachers. Meetings were recorded in order to gather the qualitative data for the study. Participant teachers also kept journals and recorded their opinions and feelings about the INSET, CFG meetings, protocols, and the classroom issues.

Waters (2006) states that ELT INSET does not always result in the desired level of 'follow-up', i.e. impact on teachers' classroom practices. He indicates that little research appears to have been carried out concerning how the design of INSET systems affects such outcomes. From the data gathered from the interviews and the journals, teachers involved in CFG appreciated the collegial environment they had been part of. They believed that by this environment, they could engage in reflective practice, which would improve the effect of the INSET programme. CFG meetings, therefore, seemed to be considered an efficient 'follow-up' by the participants. As Johnson (2009) indicates, CFGs create a structured environment where teachers can "talk through" a dilemma, collaboratively coming to understand it and seeking possible solutions. The seminars given in the INSET were on the subjects teachers need support, feedback and assistance. After each seminar, CFG members found the chance to discuss over the message of the speaker, reflected upon their opinions and tried to take the best out of the INSET organized. The design of the group enabled participant teachers to evaluate the content of the seminars and associate the outcomes with their needs and realities. The journals showed that the CFG was more than a tool to evaluate the INSET, but it was considered as a professional learning community. The CFG participants said that they built on what they learned from the INSET more than the teachers who did not participate in the CFG.

As mentioned in the theoretical framework of the study, in their professional practice, teachers are social beings in that they interact with their colleagues, learners, the curriculum in the classroom, teaching materials and tasks. From a sociocultural perspective, teacher cognition originates in and fundamentally shaped by the specific social activities in which teachers engage (Johnson, 2009). Therefore, CFG was proved to be an efficient tool to evaluate the process teachers go through before and after the INSET because as mentioned previously, both SCT and CFG assume that learning is mediated by participation in social practices and therefore a good theoretical match. All CFG participants agreed that they are a group of friends, volunteers trying to discuss reflectively to make the teaching-learning process more effective. They mentioned that the group was a place where they shared ideas, brainstormed on various topics as they anticipated. They played role in their own professional development through participating in a CFG, a collaborative model in which teachers' careful, critical and systematic examinations will be of help to themselves as well as their colleagues.

For more than a hundred years, teacher education has been based on the notion that knowledge about teaching and learning can be 'transmitted' to teachers by others especially ones who are considered experts on the area. In-service education has been the same. It has involved a relatively passive participation by teachers, while they listen to an "expert" pass on new ideas (Sparks, 1994). Now there is a shift emerging which changes the direction of staff development. Teachers have been viewed as the actors in their profession rather than the spectators.

The last research question aimed to find out if there was any change in teachers' attitudes and expectations about language teaching and learning after the INSET programme. The teachers who did not participate in CFG meetings did not have the chance to evaluate the INSET, in other words no follow-up was facilitated. The researcher asked 10 instructors, as a part of an informal interview, about the INSET organized by the institution. Whether their expectations were fulfilled or not was questioned. They stated that the INSET helped them to reconsider the issues mentioned, look at them from different perspectives, and to keep them on their agenda. However, since there was not any follow-up after each seminar, they believed that the INSET would not lead to any change in their practice. They did not have the chance to reflect on the topics discussed, or try out the suggested strategies and observe. One of the interviewees stated that the INSET seminars excited her but they were like a flash in the pan. After the seminar, she said she found herself back into usual classroom issues. Another comment was that during the INSET programme, the school functioned as a community of professionals, but it lasted just during the seminars.

The INSET programme followed by CFG offered a forum where teachers could discuss issues that were mentioned in the programme, try out new strategies discussed, get support, advice and help from other teachers in a nonthreatening environment, observe and be observed willingly, increase motivation and mutual empowerment. All participants agreed that CFG process helped them get the most out of the INSET and enabled teachers to become more aware of the complex issues involved in their teaching by sharing them with colleagues in a group.

Implications and Recommendations for Further Study

The purpose of the study was to implement a development-based INSET programme at Foreign Languages School of Mersin University and to evaluate the impact of the programme with CFG model. As mentioned before, the inquiry-based professional development models Johnson (2009) mentioned such as CFG, Peer Coaching, Lesson Study, Cooperative Development, and Teacher Study Groups define professional development as learning systematically in, from and for practice. They recognize that participation and context are essential to teacher learning, and they create conditions for teachers to engage in evidence-based learning and decision making. In this sense, CFG model was an effective tool to evaluate the impact of the INSET programme. As a matter of fact, the model was not only used as a tool for evaluation but also as it created a professional learning community. As for the implications:

1. The INSET was aimed to be organized as a five-day program, however, due to unexpected institutional constraints; it was expanded through two academic terms. All the instructors participated to the seminars, and the workshops were given by the professors from different faculties and by two instructors from the school, one being the researcher herself. The subjects considered to have a priority in the INSET programme were determined by the needs analysis as indicated in Figure 3 and 4 in Chapter 1. The concept of professional development is moving away from the practice of attending courses and training days to the concept of lifelong learning and continuing learning today. (Fraser et al., 2007). Therefore, in-service courses should be no longer perceived as short-term or one-shot programmes, given by a "professional" outside. These courses should be seen as a part of continuing education. We acknowledge that short-term workshops do not provide opportunities for teachers to make connections between the theory presented and the implications that it has for classroom teaching. These connections cannot be made without teachers taking direct role in structuring and investigating their practice. CFGs are, therefore, a valuable professional development model as teachers are given opportunities to take the time to inquire into areas of their teaching that they believe needs attention. This model validates teachers' experiences and expertise. Needs analysis should be conducted and taken into account while organizing the content and deciding on the model of professional development to be implemented.

2. The participants involved in the CFG were 6 English instructors who were volunteers and who believe in the necessity of on-going teacher development. The participants were from a variety of teaching experiences, were all women and it was their first experience to participate in such a group. Maintaining the interest, creativity, and enthusiasm of language teachers in their profession can be challenging; yet, CFG proved to be a model that fosters collaboration and reflection among teachers, increase motivation and overcome isolation. As Bayrakçı (2009) stated, giving teachers the opportunities to guide their own professional development in a flexible system will

enhance their professional approach and willingness to participate in in-service training activities. Voluntary participation should be encouraged.

3. The feasibility of applying CFG is not difficult if institutions provide necessary conditions. School administrators should provide time and space for these collaborative processes to take place. Moreover, they should be committed to empowering their staff member, because without the support and foresight of the directors, no professional development programmes will be successful. Teaching load can be decreased with a view to permitting them enough time to collaborate and cooperate with colleagues. The support of the school administration is essential.

4. When we consider the favourable results acquired in this study, we strongly believe that this research could be a starting point to support teachers' on-going learning and development process within a professional learning community. CFG model can be implemented for fostering professional development rather than a tool for evaluating a programme. Both protocols and group sessions provided opportunities for learning by creating spaces for all teachers to gain new insights into the issues being discussed. The data that were presented in Chapter 3 make a strong case that teachers liked the idea of participating in teacher support groups such as CFG because they gained much more suggestions on how to 'solve a problem', they built upon their own histories as well as the professional expertise of other group members. It is recommended that further studies should be conducted with more groups; two or three CFGs which consist of six to eight teachers during the same academic year, and this collaboration could be formalized by the school administration i.e. supporting regular monthly meetings. Teachers' tight schedule could be arranged accordingly, for example by enabling them a free afternoon in a week.

5. We claim that professional development needs to be strongly anchored in classroom practice, and CFG model accompanied with protocols is a practical and efficient way of professional development. As mentioned earlier in this dissertation, one of the goals of CFGs is to 'identify student learning goals that make sense in their schools, look reflectively at practices intended to achieve these goals, and collaboratively examine teacher and student work in order to meet that objective' (Dunne, Nave, & Lewis, 2000, p.9). CFGs provide the opportunity to work collaboratively, to delve into classroom based dilemmas, to focus on the teaching and

learning of specific academic content, and build strong working relationships among teachers. Students are the beneficiaries of this model.

6. University partnership can be supplied for future studies. CFGs can be formed in two Foreign Languages Schools in different universities, and they can act correspondingly by the help of technology. Meetings can be held via Skype, works of students can be shared by emails. Joint problems may be detected and possible solutions can be shared.

Limitations of the Study

This dissertation was intended to evaluate the impact of an INSET program which would be the first initiation aimed at proving teachers with professional development opportunities in the history of the school. However, there are some limitations. The first limitation concerns the attitude of administration. The INSET was first planned as a five-day intense INSET programme after having taken the consent of the administration. Scholars were invited from the host university as well as other institutions in Turkey. The programme was designed according to the needs analysis questionnaires and interviews applied to the instructors of the school. However, the programme was redesigned by the director of the school and the invitations were cancelled by the researcher. The school administration decided to invite scholars whom they anticipated. The INSET seminars took place approximately once a month. The instructors were informed just one or two days before the occasion. The atmosphere was not built for the INSET, and the professors invited were not directly related to English language education field. The priorities and the needs of the school and the instructors were not mentioned thoroughly to the speakers; therefore, they were not very well prepared for the seminars. However, discussion part of these presentations was the most fruitful since there was interaction between the speakers and the listeners. Some useful points were raised in this way.

Teachers participated in this study were all volunteers who were supportive and collaborative under all circumstances. They had a tight schedule and too much work load. They never missed any of the meetings, yet, they would be happier if they had some time allocated for the meetings that would help them in their professional development.

In this study, a learning community modelled after the CFG framework was implemented in a state university in Turkey. It focused on CFGs as an opportunity for professional development by examining teacher collaboration and its influence on reflective practice and teaching. Further studies should be implemented to observe the effects of CFG, a learning community model, and its impacts on teachers and students. Teachers experiencing such a journey as a critical friend should be trained as coaches. They could work with more groups aiming at an on-going teacher professional development.

The impacts of the teachers' CFG participation on students can be also examined in future studies. According to Little et. al. (2003), teachers are usually alone when they examine student work and think about student performance. CFGs have enabled teachers to leave the isolation of their own classrooms and think together about student work in the broader contexts of school improvement and professional development. So as for future studies, how examining student work by a group of teachers in a CFG affects students' performance could be investigated.

References

Allen, D. & Blythe, T. (2004). *The facilitator's book of questions: Tools for looking together at student and teacher work.* New York: Teachers College Press.

Anderson, R. K., & Hudson, J. S. (2002). *Critical Friends Groups: Collaborative inquiry for life-long learning.* Seattle, WA: Hud Anderson Enterprises.

Andreu, R., Canos, L., de Juana, S., Manresa, E., Rienda, L., & Tari, J. J. (2003). Critical friends: a tool for quality improvement in universities. *Quality Assurance in Education.* 11 (1), 31-36.

Annenberg Institute of School Reform (AISR). (2012). Retrieved from: http://annenberginstitute.org/about-us, March 23, 2010.

Armstrong, K. (2003). Advancing reflective practice and building constructive collegiality: A program's influence on teachers' experiences in urban schools. Unpublished Ed.D. Thesis, Harvard University, USA.

Atay, D. (2004). Collaborative dialogue with student teachers as a follow-up to teacher in-service education and training. *Language Teaching Research*, 8 (2), 143-162.

Atay, D. (2008). Teacher research for professional development. *ELT Journal*, 62/2, 139-147.

Avalos, B. (2011). Teacher professional development in Teaching and Teacher Education over ten years. *Teaching and Teacher Education*, 27, 10-20.

Bailey, K.M. (1992). The processes of innovation in language teacher development: What, why and how teachers change. In *J.* Flowerdew, *M.* Brock and *S.* Hsia (Eds.), *Perspectives on second language teacher education,* Hong Kong: City Polytechnic of Hong Kong, 253-282.

Bambino, D. (2002). Critical friends. *Educational Leadership*, 59 (6), 25-27.

Bayrakçı, M. (2009). In-service teacher training in Japan and Turkey: A comparative analysis of institutions and practices. *Australian Journal of Teacher Education*, 34 (1), 10-22.

Baxter, P., & Jack, S. (2008). Qualitative case study methodology: Study design and implementation for novice researchers. *The Qualitative Report,13* (4), 544-559.

Bell, B., & Gilbert, J. K. (1996). *Teacher development: A model from science education.* Routledge.

Berg, B. L. (1989). *Qualitative research methods for the social sciences*. Boston, MA: Allyn & Bacon.

Blair, R. W. (1982). *Innovative approaches to language teaching*. Rowley, MA: Newbury House.

Bloom, B. A. (1999). Critical friends groups: In pursuit of excellence. *Mt. Airy Times Express*. Retrieved from: http://www.nsrfharmony.org/mtairy.html: May 17, 2012.

Celce-Murcia, M. (1991). *Teaching English as a second or foreign language*. (2nd edition) Rowley, MA: Newbury House.

Christison, M. A., & Stoller, F. L. (Eds.) (1997). *A handbook for language program administrators*. Burlingame, CA: Alta Book Center Publishers.

Cimer, S. O., Çakır, İ., & Çimer, A. (2010). Teachers' views on the effectiveness of in-service courses on the new curriculum in Turkey. *European Journal of Teacher Education*, *33*(1), 31-41.

Clark, C. (2001). Good conversation. In *C. M.* Clark (Eds.) *Talking shop: authentic conversation and teacher learning*. New York, NY: Teachers College Press.

Clausen, K.W., Aquino, A.M., & Wideman, R. (2009). Bridging the real and ideal: A comparison between learning community characteristics and a school-based case study. *Teaching and Teacher Education,* 25, 444-452.

Coalition of Essential Schools (CES) (2008). Oakland, CA. Retrieved from: http://www.essentialschools.org, March 13, 2010.

Coalition of Essential Schools (CES) (2010). Oakland, CA. Retrieved from: http://www.essentialschools.org, March 13, 2010.

Cook, L., & Friend, M. (1995). Co-teaching: Guidelines for creating effective practices. *Focus on Exceptional Children*, 28 (3), 1-16.

Costa, A. & Kallick, B. (1993). Through the lens of a Critical Friend. *Educational Leadership*, 51(2), 49-51.

Crandall, J. A. (2000). Language teacher education. *Annual Review of Applied Linguistics*, 20, 34-55.

Creswell, J. W. (2005). Educational research: Planning, conducting, and evaluating quantitative and qualitative research (2nd edition) Upper Saddle River, NJ: Pearson//Prentice Hall.

Creswell, J.W. (2007). *Qualitative inquiry and research: Choosing among five approaches*. Thousand Oaks, CA: Sage.

Curry, M.W. (2008). Critical Friends Groups: The possibilities and limitations embedded in teacher professional communities aimed at instructional improvement and school reform. *Teachers College Record*, 110 (4), 733-774.

Cushman, K. (1996). Teacher collaboration and learning: Critical friends groups. Retrieved from: http://www.essentialschools.org: September 17, 2012.

Darling-Hammond, L. & Sykes, G. (Eds.) (1996). *Teaching as the learning profession: Handbook of policy and practice*. San Francisco: Jossey-Bass. Freeman.

Darling-Hammond, L. & Sykes, G. (2003). Wanted: A national teacher supply policy for education: The right way to meet the 'highly qualified teacher' challenge. *Educational Policy Analysis Archives*, 11 (33). Retrieved from: http://epaa.asu.edu/epaa/v11n33/: May 4, 2012.

Denzin, N. K., & Lincoln, Y. S. (2000). The discipline and practice of qualitative research. *Handbook of qualitative research*, 2, 1-28.

Doppenberg, J.J., den Brok, P.J., Bakx, A. (2012). Collaborative teacher learning across foci of collaboration: Perceived activities and outcomes. *Teaching and Teacher Education*, 28 (6), 899-910.

DuFour, R. (2004). What is a "professional learning community"? *Educational Leadership*, 61 (8), 6-11.

DuFour, R., Eaker, R. E., & DuFour, R. B. (2005). *On common ground: The power of professional learning communities*. Bloomington, IN: Solution Tree.

Duncombe, R., & Armour, K. M. (2004). Collaborative professional learning: from theory to practice. *Journal of In-service Education*, 30 (1), 141-166.

Dunne, F., Nave, B., & Lewis, A. (2000). Critical friends: Teachers helping to improve student learning. *Phi Delta Kappa International Research Bulletin*, (CEDR) (28), 9-12.

Dunne, F. & Honts, F. (1998). That group really makes me think! Critical friends groups and the development of reflective practitioners. Paper presented at the AERA Annual Meeting, San Diego, CA.

Edge, J. & Richards, K. (Eds.) (1993). *Teachers develop teachers' research*. Oxford: Heinemann.

England, L. (1998). Promoting effective professional development in English language teaching. ERIC Documents, EJ595107.

Erickson, G., Brandes, G. M., Mitchell, I. & Mitchell, J. (2005). Collaborative teacher learning: Findings from two professional development projects. *Teaching and Teacher Education,* 21 (7), 787-798.

Fishman, B. J., Marx, R. W., Best, S. and Tal, R. T. (2003). Linking teacher and student learning to improve professional development in systemic reform. *Teaching and Teacher Education*, 19 (6), 643-658.

Frankeal, J.R. & Wallen, N.E. (2000). *How to Design and Evaluate Research in Education.* New York: The McGraw-Hill.

Franzak, J. (2002). Developing a teacher identity: The impact of critical friends practice on the student teacher. *English Education*, 34 (4), 258-280.

Freeman, D. (1982). Observing teachers: Three approaches to In-service training and development. *TESOL Quarterly, 16* (1), 21-28.

Freeman, D. (1991). Three view to teachers' knowledge. *IATEFL Teacher Development Newsletter*, 1-4.

Freeman, D. (1996). Redefining the relationship between research and what teachers know. In *K. M.* Bailey & *D.* Nunan (Eds.) *Voices from the language classroom.* Cambridge: Cambridge University Press. 88-115.

Freeman, D. (1998). *Doing teacher-research: From inquiry to understanding.* Boston: Heinle & Heinle.

Freeman, D. & J. C. Richards (Eds.) (1996). *Teacher learning in language teaching.* Cambridge: Cambridge University Press.

Freeman, D. & K. E. Johnson. (1998). Reconceptualizing the knowledge base of language teacher education. *TESOL Quarterly*, 32, 397–417.

Freeman, D. (2001). Second language teacher education. In *R,* Carter & *D.* Nunan (Eds.) *The Cambridge guide to teaching English to speakers of other languages.* Cambridge: Cambridge University Press.

Fullan, M. & Stiegelbauer, S. (1991). The meaning of educational change. (2nd edition) New York: Teachers College Press.

Fullan, M. (2007). *The New Meaning of Educational Change.* Fourth Edition. New York: Teachers College Press.

Garet, M., Porter, A., Desimone, L. Birman, B., & Yoon, K. (2001). What makes professional development effective? Analysis of a national sample of teachers. *American Education Research Journal*, 38 (4), 915-945.

Gaible, E. & Burns, M. (2005). Using technology to train teachers [Online]. Retrieved from *info*DEV: http://www.infodev.org/en/Publication.13.html: 26 November, 2011.

Gindis, B. (2003). Remediation through education. In *A*. Kozulin, *B*. Gindis, *V. S*. Ageyev, & *S. M*. Miller, (Eds.), *Vygotsky's educational theory in cultural context*. Cambridge University Press: Cambridge, UK.

Güçeri, M. (2005). The impact of in-service teacher training on change agentry role of teachers and their contribution to school improvement. Unpublished Ph.D. dissertation. Middle East Technical University, Ankara, Turkey.

Hatch, J. A. (2002). *Doing qualitative research in education settings*. SUNY Press.

Hindin, A., Morocco, C. C., Mott, E. A., & Aguilar, C. M. (2007). More than just a group: Teacher collaboration and learning in the workplace. *Teachers and Teaching: theory and practice*, 13 (4), 349-376.

Holland, H. (2005). Teaching teacher: professional development to improve students' achievement. Retrieved from: www.aera.net/uploadedFiles/Journals_and_Publications: 20 July, 2011.

Hopkins, D. (1986). (Ed.) Inservice training and educational development: An international survey. Beckenham, Croom Helm, UK.

Huberman, M. (2001). Networks that alter teaching: Conceptualisations, exchanges and experiments. In *J*. Soler, *A*. Craft, & *H*. Burgess, (Eds.) *Teacher development: Exploring our own practice*. London: Paul Chapman Publishing and The Open University.

Johnson, K.E. (2009). *Second language teacher education: A sociocultural perspective*. New York: Taylor & Francis.

Johnston, B. (2003). Values in English language teaching. Mahwah, NJ: Lawrence Erlbaum.

Johnston, B. (2009). Collaborative teacher development. In *A*. Burns & *J. C*. Richards (eds.), *The Cambridge guide to language teacher education* (pp. 241-249). Cambridge: Cambridge University Press.

Kelchtermans, G. (1994). Recent European research on teacher education and professional development. In *S.* Janssens, & *R.* Loly-Smets, (Eds.) *Repport of the R.I.F.- European Symposium 93 of the Network of Teacher Training Institutions.* Leuven-Liege: RIF, UE.

Kelley, M. (2007). Critical Friends Groups: Building teacher knowledge through collaboration and reflection. NSRF Research Conference, Seattle.

Key, E. (2006). Do they make a difference? A review of research on the impact of Critical Friends Groups. A Paper Presented at the National School Reform Faculty Research Forum. Retrieved from: http://www.nsrfharmony.org: April 11, 2010

Larsen-Freeman, D. (1986). *Techniques and principles in language teaching* NY: Oxford University Pres.

Lave, J. & Wenger, E. (1991). *Situated learning: Legitimate peripheral participation.* Cambridge, UK: Cambridge University Press.

Little, J., Gearhart, M., Curry, M., & Kafka, J. (2003). Looking at student work for teacher learning, teacher community, and school reform. *Phi Delta Kappan*, 85 (3), 185-192.

Locke, L.F. (1984). Research on Teaching Teachers: Where are we now? *Journal of Teaching Physical Education*, Monograph 2.

Mann, S. (2005). The language teacher's development. *Language Teaching*, 38, 103-118.

McKenzie, M. & A. M. Carr-Reardon. (2003). 'Critical Friends Groups: FAQs about CFGs'. Available at:
http://www.city.waltham.ma.us/SCHOOL/WebPAge/cfg.htm).

McLaughlin, M.W. & Talbert, J.E. (1993). *Contexts that matter for teaching and learning.* Stanford, California: Center for Research on the Context of Secondary School Teaching, Stanford University.

McLaughlin, M. W. & Talbert, J. E. (2006). *Building school-based teacher learning communities: Professional strategies to improve student achievement.* NY: Teachers College Press

McLaughlin, M.W. (1992). What matters most in teachers' workplace context? ERIC Documents, ED342755.

Miguéns, M. (1999). INSET Teacher education through partnerships between teachers and researchers: A reflective contribution to re-exam theory and practice. Retrieved from: http://tntee.umu.se/lisboa/papers/full-papers/pdf/A7-miguens.pdf: December 12, 2011.

Miller, S. M. (2003). How literature discussion shapes thinking: ZPDs for teaching/ learning habits of the heart and mind. In *A*. Kozulin, *B*. Gindis, , *V. S*. Ageyev, , & *S. M*. Miller, (Eds.) *Vygotsky's educational theory in cultural context.* Cambridge University Press: Cambridge, UK.

National School Reform Faculty (NSRF) (2011). The Harmony Education Center, Bloomington, IN. Retrieved from: http://www.nsrfharmony.org: March 11, 2010.

Nave, B. (1998). First year evaluation report to cohort 3 schools: Preliminary analysis of data from 1997- 1998 school visits. Providence, RI: Brown University. Retrieved from http://www.nsrfharmony.org: October 5, 2011.

Nave, B. (2000). Among critical friends: A study of critical friends groups in three Maine schools. Unpublished Ed.D. dissertation, Harvard University, Massachusetts, United States.

Nefstead, K.A. (2009). Critical Friends Groups: A learning community's journey. Unpublished Ph.D. dissertation, Capella University, MN, USA. Retrieved from ProQuest Digital Dissertations database. (Publication No. UMI3359210): November 17, 2010.

Nieto, S. (2009). From surviving to thriving. *Educational leadership.* 66 (5), 8-13.

Osterman, K. & Kottkamp, R.B. (1993). *Reflective practice for educators: Improving schooling through professional development.* Newbury Park California: A Sage Publications Company.

O'Sullivan, M.C. (2001). The inset strategies model: an effective inset model for unqualified and under-qualified primary teachers in Namibia. *International Journal of Educational Development*, 21, 93-117.

Pavlenko, A. & Lantolf, J. (2000). Second language learning as participation and the (re) construction of Selves. In *J. P.* Lantolf (Ed.), *Sociocultural theory and second language learning: Recent advances* (pp.155–177). New York: Oxford University Press.

Peterson-Veatch, R. (2007). CFGs and Transformation: An Emergent Theory of Action. *NSRF Research Forum.*

Pettis, J. (2002). Developing our professional competence. In Richards & Renandya (eds.), *Methodology in Language Teaching: An Anthology of Current Practice.* (388–392) NY: Cambridge University Press.

Poehner, M.P. 2009. Drafting a new chapter on critical friends groups: Exploring teacher learning from a Vygotskian perspective. PhD dissertation. Pennsylvania State University, USA. Retrieved from ProQuest Digital Dissertations database. (Publication No. UMI3374533).

Richards, J.C. & T. S. Rodgers. (1982). Method: Approach, design and procedure. *TESOL Quarterly*, 16, 153–168.

Richards, J.C. (1990). Beyond training: approaches to teacher education in language teaching. *The Language Teacher*, 14, 3-8.

Richards, J. & Lockhart, C. (1994). *Reflective teaching in second language classrooms.* Cambridge: Cambridge University Press.

Richards, J. C. (1998). *Beyond Training.* Cambridge: CUP.

Richards, J. C. & Farrell, T. C. (2005). *Professional development for language teachers.* New York: Cambridge University Press.

Roberts, J. (1998). *Language Teacher Education.* London: Arnold.

Rosenholtz, S. (1989). *Teacher's workplace: the social organization of schools.* New York: Longman.

Saito, H. & Ebsworth, M. E. (2004). Seeing English Language Teaching and Learning through the Eyes of Japanese EFL and ESL Students. *Foreign Language Annal*, 37 (1), 111.

Şahin, V. (2006). Evaluation of the In-service teacher training program "The Certificate for Teachers of English" at the Middle East Technical University School of Foreign Languages. Unpublished PhD. dissertation, Middle East technical University, Ankara, Turkey.

Şeker, M. (2007). Exploring effects of collaborative learning in enhancing teachers' development in teaching English to young learners. Unpublished Ph.D. dissertation, Çukurova University, Adana, Turkey.

Snow-Gerono, J. L. (2005). Professional development in a culture of inquiry: PDS teachers identify the benefits of professional learning communities. *Teaching and Teacher Education*, 21, 241-256.

Sparks, D. (1994). A paradigm shift in staff development. *Education Week, Forum, 42.*

Stevick, E. W. (1980). *Teaching languages: A way and ways.* Rowley, MA: Newbury House.

Stevick, E. W. (1998). *Working with teaching methods: What's at stake?* Boston: Heinle and Heinle.

Stoll, L. & Louis, K. S. (2007). Professional learning communities: Elaborating new approaches. *Professional learning communities: Divergence, depth and dilemmas*, 1-13.

Stoll, L., Bolam, R., McMahon, A., Wallace, M. & Thomas, S. (2006). Professional learning communities: A review of the literature. *Journal of educational change*, 7 (4), 221-258.

Theunissen, M. & Veenman, S. (1998). *Interorganizational networks in the domain of in-service teacher training.* ERIC Document Reproduction Service, No. ED 421468

Underhill, A. (1999). Continuous teacher development. *IATEFL Issues*, 149, 14-18.

Ur, P. (1996). *A Course in Language Teaching.* Cambridge: Cambridge, University Press.

Ur, P. (2002). The English teacher as professional. In *J.C.*, Richards, & *W. A.*, Renandya, (Eds.). *Methodology in Language Teaching: An Anthology of Current Practice.* NY: Cambridge University Press.

Uysal, H. H. (2012). Evaluation of an In-service Training Program for Primary-school Language Teachers in Turkey. *Australian Journal of Teacher Education,37*(7), 2.

Villegas-Reimers, E. (2003). Teacher professional development: An international review of the literature. OECD report, Paris: International Institute for Educational Planning.

Vo, L.T. & Nguyen, H.T.M. (2010). Critical Friends Group for EFL teacher professional development. *ELT Journal,* 64 (2), 205-213.

Vygotksy, L. S. (1978). Mind in society: The development of higher psychological processes (M. Cole, V. John-Steiner, S. Scribner, & E. Souberman, Eds.). Cambridge, MA: Harvard University Press.

Wallace, M. (1991). *Training foreign language teachers: a reflective approach.* Cambridge: Cambridge University Press.

Waters, A. (2006). Facilitating follow-up in ELT INSET. *Language Teaching Research,* 10 (1), 32-52.

Wells, G. (2000). Dialogic inquiry in education. *Vygotskian Perspectives on Literacy Research*, 51-85.

Widdowson, H.G. (1997). Approaches to second language teacher education. In *G. R.* Tucker & *D.* Corson (eds.) *Encyclopedia of language and education, Volume 4. Second language education.* Dordrecht, Netherlands: Kluwer. 121–129.

Willams, M. & Burden, R. (1997). *Psychology for Language Teachers*. Cambridge: Cambridge University Press.

Williams, M. L. (2010). Teacher Colloboration as Professional Development in a Large, Suburban High School. PhD dissertation. University of Nebraska, USA.

Wilson, S. M. & Berne, J. (1999). Teacher Learning and the Acquisition of Professional Knowledge: An Examination of Research on Contemporary Professional Development. *Review of Research in Education*, 24, 173.

Woodward, T. (1991). *Models and metaphors in language teacher training: Loop input and other strategies*. Cambridge: Cambridge University Press.

Yin, R. K. (1994). *Case study research design and methods* (2nd ed.). Thousand Oaks, CA: Sage.

Zeichner, K., & Noffke, S. (2001). Practitioner research. In *V.* Richardson (Ed.), *Handbook of research on teaching* (4th edition, 314-330). Washington, DC: American Educational Research Association.

Appendices

Appendix A. Dissertations on CFGs

	Focus Questions	Population	Summary of Findings
		Dissertations	
Theiss (1998)	Are there differences in teachers' perceptions and practices over time as a result of participation in CFGs?	CFGs at eight suburban schools involved in reform initiatives	Due to inconsistencies between survey and interview data, results of this study are inconclusive. However, Theiss asserts that these CFGs did become collaborative communities and that reflection served to help group members build norms and share knowledge. On the other hand, there was little evidence of the kind of critical reflection that leads to change and growth. Theiss suggests that real change takes time, and that perhaps a two year time period is not long enough to see real change occur.
Nave (2000)	How do CFGs develop over time? Does the thinking and practice of CFG participants change over time? If so, how? A test of the NSRF theory of action.	An elementary, middle, and high school from NSRF cohort three	Nave reports that CFGs do develop into collegial communities with collegial interaction outside of group meetings. He found evidence for changes in teacher thinking, changes in teacher practice, and improvements in student achievement. Factors supporting these changes include faithful implementation of the CFG program, a skilled coach, a principal who models inquiry, the commitment of members, and a supportive school context. He asserts that a higher degree of CFG implementation yields greater changes in teachers.
Murphy (2001)	From the perspectives of various stakeholders, what internal or external factors support or hinder the work of CFGs in large urban high schools? What aspects of the implementation effort may have contributed to the failure to sustain?	CFGs in one urban high school	Though Murphy identifies several factors that supported the work of CFGs (voluntary participation, trust, collective responsibility, collegial discourse, etc.), she identifies numerous hindrances that ultimately led to the elimination of CFGs from one high school after five years of implementation. Changes in district level administration, an isolated and top-down school culture, district focus on accountability, coach burn-out, attempts to create too many groups all at once, and participants' rejection of peer observations acted as barriers to CFG work. Murphy also found that without a focused goal, CFG activities were highly disconnected. Participants were more focused on the process than the content.
Nay (2002)	Does involvement in a CFG create opportunities for professional growth? Do teachers adapt and change their classroom practice as a result of their participation in a CFG?	One CES high school's CFG	Nay concludes that CFGs do provide opportunities for professional growth and that teachers do change their practice as a result of participation. However, evidence cited in the study points to small cosmetic changes in teaching, such as a revised rubric, rather than significant learning, growth, or transformation of practice.
Armstrong (2003)	What was the experience of reflective practice and	CFGs at three urban CES	Though all participants in this research study were satisfied with their CFG

		high schools	experience, there was considerable variation in CFGs across schools. Armstrong found that CFG participation did move teachers a step further along a collegiality continuum, but that the initial school culture may have been a constraint on forging even deeper collegial ties. The program itself was weak in supporting rigor in reflective practice. Success depended upon the quality of questions raised and the level of willingness to be challenging and truthful. Armstrong concluded that success in a CFG depends on the degree to which group participants are able to keep the program meaningful and rigorous.
Curry (2003)	How are CFGs a resource for school reform and professional development?	Six CFGs in a CES high school	This case study indicates that CFGs both enable and constrain school culture for instructional improvement and school reform. CFGs promote collegial ties across departments, curricular coherence, and a school-wide orientation. However, the micropolitics of reform hindered full participation in CFGs, intensifying debates and schisms. Though the staff preferred CFGs to other forms of staff development, CFGs in this context lacked the depth, continuity, and coherence and robustness. The staff's interest in participation waned as they perceived diminishing returns over time. Therefore, the author concludes that CFGs were insufficient as a resource for transforming this high school.
Seaford (2003)	Do CFGs contribute to the development of learning organizations? Do schools with CFGs exhibit the five learning disciplines?	CFGs in CES schools	Seaford examines CFGs through the lens of organizational development, particularly Peter Senge's five learning disciplines of systems thinking, team learning, shared vision, personal mastery, and mental models. Data from this study indicate that both CES schools and CFGs develop these five learning disciplines, but that it may be easier to do so within a CFG than school-wide. CFG coaches reported that their CFGs exhibited all five of these disciplines to a very great extent, with systems thinking the greatest and mental models the lowest. Seaford found a significant difference between the manifestation of the five disciplines in CES schools and their CFGs, with the CFGs ranking higher. On the other hand, the data indicated no significant difference between the manifestation of the five disciplines in a first year CFG schools and those with two or more years of CFG work.
Van Soelen (2003)	What happens when novice teachers participate in a CFG? How do they make sense of 1st year experiences? How do they make decisions about teaching & learning?	Novice teachers	This CFG functioned as a mentoring community for novice teachers, a community with reciprocal rather than hierarchical relationships. Rather than those topics traditionally used in induction programs for novice teachers (like classroom management), these teachers engaged in discussions of

			curriculum, assessment, and motivation, topics stemming from their own interests and authentic work and that indicate they have surpassed Fuller's initial stages of teacher development. These novice teachers were able to provide multiple perspectives, give feedback for decision-making, and enrich each other's thinking as agents of change for one another. However, putting learning into practice was more difficult than learning to see or think in a new way.
Nefstead (2009)	What were the initial perceptions of the participants in terms of their definitions of a professional learning community? How did the use of Critical Friends Groups change teachers' perceptions of their school as a professional learning community? What changes in teachers' instructional strategies occurred as a result of their participation in CFGs?	Teachers from Kindergarten through tenth grade in an international school in Ulaanbaatar	Nefstead conducted the study in Ulaanbaatar with 36 Mongolian teachers, so it represents data out of the U.S. This study focused on CFGs as an opportunity to study teacher collaboration and its influence on reflective practice and teaching. The information obtained from the research validated the effectiveness of CFGs in giving teachers different perspectives on their own pedagogy. The data indicated that the teachers used their CFG meeting time about ways to improve their teaching and their student's learning. Changes in the way participants thought about their teaching were observed. Finally, the data indicated there was improved student learning among students whose teachers seem to have changed during the study.
Poehner (2009)	How can a Vygotskian theoretical framework contribute to our understanding of teacher learning within the context of CIGs (Conversation as Inquiry Groups)? How do the presenting teachers in CIGs work through their dilemma of practice? How does the selection and use of a specific protocol (tool) that is used in the CIG process mediate the presenting teachers' learning?	Two teachers who enrolled a course through the Professional Development School in an Atlantic university.	The study examines teacher development, as it emerges through participation in CIGs, from the perspective of Vygotsky's Sociocultural Theory. Two protocols were used for the study, namely Consultancy Protocol and Describing Student Work Protocol. As for the findings, researcher states that the teachers were engaged in more than just reconceptualising their dilemma-they also made significant changes to their practice after their involvement in the CIG process. The mediation through participating in CIG helped position the teachers to transform aspects of their classroom practice to reflect the new knowledge they co-constructed during CIG. According to the results of the study, the teachers gained much more suggestions on how to 'solve a problem' - they built upon their own histories as well as the professional expertise of their CIG members to chart a new path that included not only a new orientation to the original dilemma but also ideas for how to engage other learners in their classrooms.

Note: From Key, E. (2006). Do they make a difference? A review of research on the impact of Critical Friends Groups. A Paper Presented at the National School Reform Faculty Research Forum. Retrieved from: http://www.nsrfharmony.org: April 11, 2010

Appendix B. Charrette Protocol

Original written by Kathy Juarez, Piner High School, Santa Rosa, California.
Revised by Gene Thompson-Grove, January 2003, NSRF.
Revised by Kim Feicke, October 2007, NSRF.

The following list of steps attempts to formalize the process for others interested in using it.

1. A team or an individual requests a charrette when:
a. the team/individual is experiencing difficulty with the work,
b. a stopping point has been reached, or
c. additional minds (thinkers new to the work) could help move it forward.

2. A group, ranging in size from three to six people, is formed to look at the work. A moderator/facilitator is designated from the newly formed group. It is the moderator's job to observe the charrette, record information that is being created, ask questions along the way, and occasionally summarize the discussion.

3. The requesting team/individual presents its "work in progress" while the group listens. (There are no strict time limits, but this usually takes five or ten minutes.) Sometimes, the invited group needs to ask two or three clarifying questions before moving on to Step 4.

4. The requesting team/individual states what it needs or wants from the charrette, thereby accepting responsibility for focusing the discussion. This focus is usually made in the form of a specific request, but it can be as generic as "How can we make this better?" or "What is our next step?"

5. The invited group then discusses while the requesting team/individual listens and takes notes. There are no hard and fast rules here. Occasionally (but not usually) the requesting team/individual joins in the discussion process. The emphasis is on improving the work, which now belongs to the entire group. The atmosphere is one of "we're in this together," and our single purpose is "to make a good thing even better."

6. When the requesting team/individual knows it has gotten what it needs from the invited group, they stop the process, briefly summarize what was gained, thank the participants and moderator and return to the "drawing board."

7. Debrief the process as a group.

Appendix C. Needs Analysis Questionnaire

Dear Colleagues,

This questionnaire will highlight your attitudes towards in-service education and training (INSET) programmes, and inform the researcher about your needs for the INSET programme which is planned for the School of Foreign Languages. Your contribution will be of great help to the researcher in the design and implementation phase of the course. All responses will be treated with extreme confidentiality. Thank you for your cooperation.

Nafiye Çiğdem Aktekin

Background Information:

Name/ Surname:

Gender (please circle):   Female   Male

Years of Teaching Experience:

Your highest educational qualification:

Bachelor's Degree (BA)   Masters Degree (MA)   Doctorate Degree (PhD)

1. **Have you ever participated in any in-service training activities?**
   Yes   **No**

If 'Yes',

When:

Where:

By Whom:

2. **To what extent was the training you received helpful in your professional development?**

   To no extent   1   2   3   4   5   To a very large extent

3. **What activities do you follow for your own professional development? (Seminars, workshops, recent articles, etc.)**

4. Do you think you need an INSET programme designed for your School?
  Yes   **No**

If 'No', explain the reason:

5. What would be the benefit of an INSET programme for your own development?

6. Which direction of activities is believed to be prior in your school? (Mark 3 of them)

_____ Improving foreign language skills

_____ Improving quality of education

_____ Promoting co-operation in education (institutions in and out of the university)

_____ Supporting teachers development

_____Working on educational innovations and original educational programmes

_____ Promoting use of computer and informative techniques

_____ Supporting student motivation for learning

_____ Supporting teacher motivation

_____ Introducing new methods and forms of teaching

Others:
....

7. What are your expectations concerning the effects of the INSET?

The INSET may

_____ improve my students' knowledge

_____ improve and renovate my knowledge

_____ enable me to get new skills

_____ upgrade my existing skills

_____ provide opportunities to exchange experience and views

_____ add additional qualifications

_____ inform me about educational innovations

_____ help me reflect on my teaching practices

_____ increase my motivation

_____ expand the conceptual understanding of my teaching

Please specify any other expectations:
....
....
....
....

8. In what areas do you think you need training and education? Please specify:

Thank you very much!

Appendix D. Presentation about CFG Study

Critical Friends Group
at Mersin University
School of Foreign Languages

Nafiye Çiğdem Aktekin
13.10.2010

What is Critical Friends Group?

* A CFG is composed of peers where there is no 'hierarchy of expertise' and it must support a democratic, reflective, and collaborative community of learners.

* A CFG is a voluntary group of teachers who meet together regularly to support one another's personal and professional development through critical analysis of theories and ideas, new and existing practices, and student and teacher work.

Critical	Friends
• Linked to student learning	• Based on respect and genuine listening
• Vehicle for professional growth; growing together	• Working as a team
• Ongoing, interactive	• Neither judgmental nor evaluative
• Goal oriented, student achievement & success	• Both reflective and collaborative

Critical Friends

Who developed the CFG concept?

* CFGs were born out of the Annenberg Institute for School Reform in 1994.

* Shortly after the program was designed, The National School Reform Faculty, the professional development wing of the Institute, began to train coaches in a program that was both "practioner-driven and highly collaborative"

Why conduct CFG?

* To have in-dept, insightful conversations about teaching and learning
* To provide deliberate time and structures to promote adult professional growth that is linked to student learning
* Increase student learning through ongoing support for teachers in a small colloborative group setting

Working in a small group...

* To share activities and ideas to foster a sense of common purpose
* To honor differences in its members' styles of teaching and learning
* Teachers identify their individual professional needs

Sociocultural perspective of CFG

* Learning to teach is based on the assumption that knowing, thinking and understanding come from participating in the social practices of learning and teaching in specific classroom and school situations.

(Johnson, 2009)

What is a Protocol?

* A protocol consists of agreed upon **guidelines for a conversation**
  -- which everyone understands and has agreed to
  -- that permits a certain kind of conversation to occur
  -- often a kind of conversation which people are not in the habit of having

* Protocols are vehicles for **building the skills and culture necessary for collaborative work.**

What does it take?

* Time
* Trust
* Respect
* Commitment
* Belief in the process

Change is inevitable...

Growth is optional.

Appendix E. Participant Consent Form

You are being asked to read the following material to ensure that you are informed of the nature of the research study and of how you will participate in it, if you consent to do so.

Purpose: The purpose of the study is to evaluate the impact of inservice teacher education (INSET) programme on professional development of EFL teachers through the critical friends group (CFG).

Selection Criteria: You are being invited to participate in the above titled research project because you are a volunteer member of a Critical Friends Group.

Participation and Subject Compensation: There is no cost to participate in this study. Participation in meetings (8 in one term), and completion of a journal will consume approximately three hours of your time in a month. You will be asked to fill in a survey and a questionnaire. You will observe and will be observed by another participant once. The meetings and the observations will be recorded and /or video-taped. You will not be compensated for your participation.

Benefits: Participants will work in a small group setting (CFG) to promote their professional growth in a collaborative and reflective environment. You will benefit cognitively and emotionally from engaging in self-reflection about your teaching as well as your social interaction in a Critical Friends Group. Information derived from the meetings, observations will provide insight into your teaching career. Being part of an educational research is an advantage and can be added to your resume.

Risks: There are no foreseeable risks of participation in this project.

Confidentiality: The findings of the study may be published; individual participants will not be identified. The transcripts data will be kept confidential. The principal investigator will be the only individual who has access to this data.

Contact: You can obtain further information about the study by contacting the investigator, Nafiye Çiğdem Aktekin, at 0532 591 7679 or email me at nafiyecigdem@gmail.com.

Authorization: Before giving my consent and signing this form, the methods, inconveniences, risks, and benefits have been explained to me, and my questions have been answered. I may ask questions at any time and I am free to withdraw from the project at any time without causing bad feeling. This consent form will be filed in a secure area with access restricted to the investigator, Nafiye Çiğdem Aktekin. I do not give up any of my legal rights by signing this form.

I have read and understood the above information and voluntarily agree to participate in the research project described above.

_____ _____
Participant's Signature   Date

Investigator's Affidavit: I have carefully explained to the participant the nature of the above project. I hereby certify that to the best of my knowledge the person who is signing this form clearly understands the nature, demands, and benefits that are involved in his/her participation and his/her signature is legally valid.
Signature of Investigator_____ Date _____

Appendix F. Agenda Template

The School of Foreign Languages

Critical Friends Group Meeting

Members Present: Aslı Güler, Selvin Güven, Tuba Dinç, Sayeste Dora, Suna Aksoy, Aynur Yüksel		
Date: 16/3/2010 Time: 14:45/16:30 Location: School of F. L Room 406		
Agenda Items	**Notes**
1. Consent Form Guidelines for the journal Reflective Questions	– Collected from all participants
2. Success Analysis Protocol	The group told to think about the best practice they've applied within this month. They complained
3.	about the loaded syllabus still there are some practice shared.
Learning Stysles (VAK) questionnaire is given and TS will apply it in their classrooms. Turkish translation will be supplied Journal entries will be collected every week.		

Next CFG –
   Time: 30/03/20
   Location: Room 406		

Appendix G. Observation Protocol

OBSERVATION PROTOCOL

TEAMING

In the "Interesting Moments" protocol, the debriefing process became more of a shared activity – both participants searching for some understanding, trying to create meaning. In this version, the participants also share the planning and implementation of the lesson(s) that is to be taught. Utilizing a form of parallel teaching or a more seamless co-teaching, the participants are both "on" with the students. Both are observers; both are observed.

Pre-Observation Conference

This takes the form of a planning session. Issues of outcomes, goals, objectives, and assessment are discussed and the activity is planned. If the two participants will be co-teaching and one or both are unfamiliar with the art of teaching with a partner, special attention should be paid to the issue of who will do what and how they will interact when working with the students.

Observation

It is important that some form of observational notes is taken. In a co-teaching situation, some people carry a clipboard or notebook as they move around the classroom, taking time to note anything of interest. Others feel this distracts them (or their students) and prefer to write as soon as possible after the event. A third method would be to videotape the session and use the playback during the debriefing. *(Warning: the use of video needs to be considered carefully. Among other considerations, it creates the need for a longer debriefing period.)*

Debriefing

As with the "Interesting Moments" protocol, either participant begins by raising a point of interest, stating as clearly and as fully as possible what occurred. A conversation develops around the interest with both observer and observed attempting to sort out, "What was going on there?"

Appendix H. HOW TO KEEP THE JOURNAL

Date:

Reflections from the meetings:

What did you share with the group?

What did other members share with the group?

What do you think you have learnt from this experience?

Reflections from your class:

What was good about the week?

What was bad about the week?

What would you like to share with the group about the week?

Is anything learnt from the meetings that you can apply in the classroom? Explain.

Reflections from the INSET:

So What?
Interpretation
What was significant to you? Why? What inferences can you make about what we did or why we did it this way?

Now What?
Application
How might I use this with my Critical Friends Group or in my classroom? What would I do differently?

Appendix I. Some Data Examples

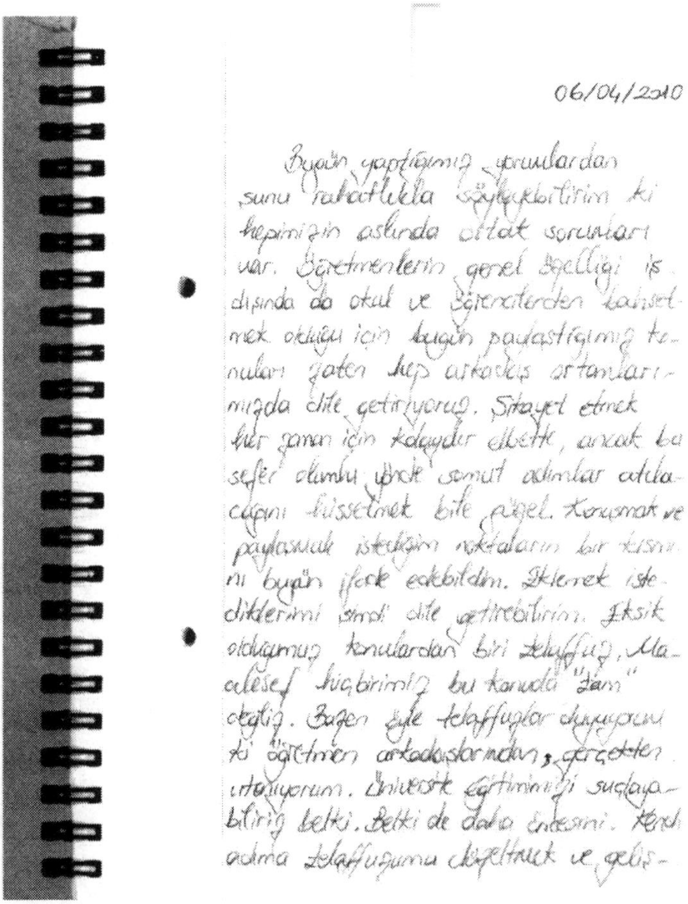

06/04/2010

Bugün yaptığımız yorumlardan
şunu rahatlıkla söyleyebilirim ki
hepimizin aslında ortak sorunları
var. Öğretmenlerin genel özelliği iş
dışında da okul ve öğrencilerden bahset-
mek olduğu için bugün paylaştığımız ko-
nuları zaten hep arkadaş ortamları-
mızda dile getiriyoruz. Şikayet etmek
her zaman için kolaydır elbette, ancak bu
sefer olumlu yönde somut adımlar atıla-
cağını hissetmek bile güzel. Konuşmak ve
paylaşmak istediğim noktaların bir kısmı-
nı bugün ifade edebildim. Ekleyerek iste-
diklerimi şimdi dile getirebilirim. Eksik
olduğumuz konulardan biri telaffuz. Ma-
alesef hiçbirimiz bu konuda "tam"
değiliz. Bazen öyle telaffuzlar duyuyorum
ki öğretmen arkadaşlarımdan, gerçekten
utanıyorum. Üniversite eğitimimizi suçlaya-
biliriz belki. Belki de daha öncesini. Kendi
adıma telaffuzumu düzeltmek ve geliş-

Reflection Questions

1) Onlarca yıldır farklı kurum ve kuruluşlarda çalışır, farklı yaş gruplarına dil öğretmediğim yapmama rağmen halen öğretmen. Ne adına öğrenebileceğim çok şey olduğuna inanıyorum. Gerek İngilizce dilbilgisi ve gerekse dil becerilerini öğretirken tecrübenin önemli olduğu kanısındayım. İşte bu tecrübe ve gereksinimlerimizi tamamlamamız için fikir alış veriş yapabileceğimiz Critical Friends Group'a ihtiyacımız vardır. Hiçbir haz- rans olmaksızın; birbirimize ders verirde; ders hazırlanırken bütün bu öğretim sürecinde karşılaştığımız zorlukları) fikirleri; tecrübe- leri paylaşmamız sağlamak- tadır. Son derece yararlı ve

(1)

gerekli olduğu kanısındayım.

2) "Critical Friends Group"ın üzerimde olumlu etkileri oldu.
— Birlikte çalıştığım meslek- taşlarımın derslerdeki
uç 3 olduğu yöntem ve tekniği dil öğretimiyle ilgili görüşle- rini öğrenme fırsatı buldum.

— Karşılaştığım problemleri birlikte tartışarak çözme ola- nağım oldu.

— Arkadaşlardan farklı oyun ve şarkı vs. gibi materyal- ler edinebildim.

3) Örneğin, pronunciation'a derste zaman yetmediği için az vakit ayırıyordum. Fakat

(2)

"VAK Learning Styles" testi verilir.

⇒ Dersi daha etkili yapmak ve motivasyon artırmak için ekstra materyaller götürülmeli.

⇒ VAK (Self-Assessment Questionnaire)'le öğrencilerin öğrenme stilleri hakkında bilgi edinilir.

⇒ Gelecek toplantıda anket sorularını arkadaşlarımla paylaşmak.

⇒ Listening'de uyguladığım ve aklıma takılan metodu anlatmak.

④

:)

---

arkadaşım Sinan'ın fikri olan "problematic sounds"ları öğrencilere sağladığı yarar, duygularında; sınıfta pronunciation öğretiminin daha çok önemsedim.

⇒ Group toplantısında)

"Pronunciation"ın önemi

- Uyguladığım syllabus'ın çok hızlı olması; bu nedenle dersin tekdüze ve sıkıcı geçmesi ⇒ Bu sıkıntıların yani true ve syllabus'ı geliştirme becerime aktarılması.

"Peripheral Learning"ın önemi; sınıf ve koridorların ders materyalleri ile donatılması. Ör: Cards, pictures

③

Appendix J. Success Analysis Protocol

SUCCESS ANALYSIS PROTOCOL
Developed by Daniel Baron, NSRF.

Roles

A timekeeper/a facilitator

Steps

1. Reflect on and write a short description of the "Best Practice" of your CFG. Note what it is about the practice that makes it so successful. (5 minutes)

2. In groups of 4, the first person shares their CFGs' "Best Practice" and why it is so successful.
(3-5 minutes)

3. The group of 4 discusses how this practice is different than other CFG practices. (3-5 minutes)

4. Each of the other three members of the group shares their CFGs' "Best Practice" and why it is so successful, followed by a group discussion analyzing how this practice differs from other CFG practices. (Each round should take 6-10 minutes)

5. The small group discusses what was learned by the analysis and what the implications for other CFG work are. (10 minutes)

6. Debrief the protocol and write four "CFG Best Practice" headlines on one piece of chart paper.
(5 minutes)

Appendix K. Conducting a Constructivist Tuning Protocol for Examining Student Work

CONSTRUCTIVIST TUNING PROTOCOL

1. Introduction

Facilitator briefly introduces protocol goals, norms, and agenda. (3 minutes)

2. Presentation
The presenter has 10 minutes to present the student's work to the participants. Place the work in context in regards to the course, the assignment, and the student. Be sure to present the "essential qualities" your students are working towards. Allow time for participants to assess the student's work. No interruptions or questions are allowed, just listening and note taking by the participants. (10 minutes)

3. Clarifying questions (3 minutes)

4. Reflection
Participants take a few minutes to review notes and to reflect on what feedback they can give that would be most helpful to the presenter. (5 minutes)

5. Warm Feedback
Participants share the evidence they found of the "essential qualities" present in the work. Presenter may only listen and take notes while participants talk. (5 minutes)

6. Cool Feedback
Participants share questions that arise addressing the lack of evidence of "essential qualities" in the student's work. Suggestions for constructive feedback to the student are appropriate. Presenter may only listen and take notes while participants talk. (5 minutes)

7. Review Feedback
Presenter takes a few minutes to review the feedback and to consider his/her response. (2-3 minutes)

8. Presenter's Response
Presenter responds to those comments and questions that he or she chooses to. Participants are silent. (5 minutes)

9. Debriefing
Talk about the process of tuning the presentation. What frustrations or positive reactions were experienced? What applications might there be for student peer or self-assessment? (5-10 minutes)

Appendix L. Dilemma's Protocol

Framing Consultancy Dilemmas
and Consultancy Questions
Developed in the field by educators affiliated with NSRF.

1. Think about your dilemma.
Dilemmas deal with issues with which you are struggling or that you are unsure about.
Some criteria for a dilemma might include:
• Is it something that is bothering you enough that your thoughts regularly return to the dilemma?
• Is it an issue/dilemma that is not already on its way to being resolved?
• Is it an issue/ dilemma that does not depend on getting other people to change (in other words, you can affect the dilemma by changing your practice)?
• Is it something that is important to you, and is it something you are actually willing to work on?

2. Do some reflective thinking about your dilemma.
Some questions that might help are:
• Why is this a dilemma for you?
• Why is this dilemma important to you?
• If you could take a snapshot of this dilemma, what would you/we see?
• What have you done already to try to remedy or manage the dilemma?
• What have been the results of those attempts?
• Who do you hope changes? Who do you hope will take action to resolve this dilemma? If your answer is *not* you, you need to change your focus. You will want to present a dilemma that is about *your* practice, actions, behaviors, beliefs, and assumptions, and *not* someone else's.
• What do you assume to be true about this dilemma, and how have these assumptions influenced your thinking about the dilemma?
• What is your focus question? A focus question summarizes your dilemma and helps focus the
feedback (see the next step).

3. Frame a focus question for your Consultancy group:
Put your dilemma into question format.
• Try to pose a question around the dilemma that seems to get to the heart of the matter.
• Remember that the question you pose will guide the Consultancy group in their discussion of the dilemma.

4. Critique your focus question.
• Is this question important to my practice?
• Is this question important to student learning?
• Is this question important to others in my profession?

5. As part of your preparation for your Consultancy, ask your facilitator or a colleague to help you refine your thinking about your dilemma and focus question by asking you a few clarifying and probing questions.
Appendix M. Lesson Observation Checklist

LESSON OBSERVATION CHECKLIST

Name of Teacher: **Name of Observer:**

Date of Observation: **Length of Lesson:**

Class/Level: **# Students:**

1. **Objectives:** What were the objectives of the lesson? Were they clear, specific and appropriate to the level? Was the lesson agenda on the board and/or stated in the weekly course outline? Do you think the specified objectives were achieved?

2. **Lesson Structure:** Did the lesson progress through clear stages (engage, study, activate, wrap-up). What happened during each stage?

3. **Communication:** How did the teacher use their voice, clarity, 'level-appropriate' speed? Were instructions clear? Was modelling and elicitation used where appropriate? How did the teacher ensure that students understood explanations/instructions?

4. **Teaching Material:** What kind of material was used? Was there a variety of aids, such as texts, handouts, realia, video, etc.?

5. **Classroom Rapport:** What was the 'mood' or atmosphere of the class? Was there good rapport between student-teacher and students-students? How did the teacher demonstrate sensitivity to students' learning difficulties?

6. **Student Participation:** Were all students engaged and involved in various stages of the lesson? Were student-student and student-teacher interactions managed effectively? Were the students motivated and interested throughout the lesson? What was the ratio of teacher talking time to students talking time? Was this appropriate?

7. **Activities:** What kind of activities did you observe? Was there a variety of activities planned and used? Did the pace from activity to activity seem appropriate?

8. **Monitoring and Error Correction:** What kinds of techniques were used to check students learning; comprehension check questions, usage check questions, etc.? Was there variety of correction techniques? Did students seem comfortable with correction?

Comments:

Appendix N. Researcher's Notes

Aynur
Asl
Tuba
Selvin
Sina
me!
sayeste

The School of Foreign Languages

Notes from CFG Meetings: 19.10.2011

All members present!

Friends are tired, but they seem happy to be together. After tea & cookies, the week was evaluated.

"I am tired of trying to catch up the syllabus. I am still behind it. I've told my partner but she isn't happy." (Tuba)

Sayeste also seemed exhausted. She complained about the environment in the testing unit. "When I go home, I (atmosphere) even couldn't find energy to deal with my son."

The group was introduced the "Dilemmas Protocol". Selvin "We need to think about it a little." Asl. "which one will I tell? I'm full of dilemmas."

"Ok, then! "Since we have cookies in this meeting, let's warm-up by "Fortune cookie warm-up". (The researcher) Participants took a cookie and assumed that there was "fortune" written in it for them. They were asked how this "fortune" might relate to them and their work. After some time, friends read the "fortune" out loud. Anything they wished to be true about their work. Cookies were eaten then! ☺

" Thank you, I feel better now!" Sayeste > She is still hopeless about her fortune will come true, she asked for understanding and kind management staff.
Back to Dilemma's protocol. Key words:
⟹

Made in the USA
San Bernardino, CA
01 August 2016